Essays on Design 1

Design: David Hillman & Jane Chipchase
Pentagram Design Limited

Editor: Robyn Marsack
Assistant Editors: Vicky Hayward & Liz Farrelly

Copyright © 1997 Booth-Clibborn Editions
Text and images copyright © 1997 the authors of the essays

The text and images in this book have been supplied by the authors
concerned. Whilst every effort has been made to ensure accuracy,
Booth-Clibborn Editions does not accept responsibility for errors
or omissions.

First published in 1997 by
Booth-Clibborn Editions
12 Percy Street London W1P 9FB

ISBN: 1-873968-24-8

All rights reserved under international copyright convention. No
part of this publication may be reproduced, stored in a retrieval
system or transmitted in any form or by any means, electronic,
mechanical, photocopying, recording, or otherwise, without
prior permission in writing from Booth-Clibborn Editions and
the copyright owners.

Printed and bound in Hong Kong

Essays on Design 1
AGI's Designers of Influence

Booth-
Clibborn
Editions

Contents

CHAPTER 3

THE SOCIAL ROLE OF THE DESIGNER

Introduction

The Alliance Graphique Internationale (AGI) was founded in 1951. It soon attracted leading exponents of graphic design in Europe and the USA, who responded to the idea of sharing common interests and friendships across national and cultural borders. Over five decades, this elite club has grown, and today there are over 240 members from America, Australia, Asia, the Middle East and Europe. They have been responsible for the identity design of most of the world's top corporations, and for countless examples of packaging, publications, illustration and posters familiar to many people around the world.

AGI membership requires reputation and achievement of the highest order. Through the relationships and interaction of its members, it promotes graphic design in lectures, education and publishing. It encourages knowledge among the young and fosters contacts with other institutions, organisations and companies. It remains dedicated to internationalism in graphic design as a means of communication and information.

In Designers of Influence, the AGI confirms its commitment to the processes of visual learning and perception unfettered by cultural differences. With appreciation and analysis, homage is paid to the talent and style of many of the truly great exponents of graphic design, often by those who are themselves among the most respected in their field. Didactic approaches and discursive views are given on design education, and the relevance of graphic design in society is explored and explained.

The essays have been collected from a variety of sources. Some were not initially intended for publication, others have been translated and may have lost some of their original nuances. Essays that started out as lectures have not been edited and retain their original form.

David Gibbs

CHAPTER 1

Personalities and People

Saul Bass
Pieter Brattinga
Alan Fletcher
Henry Wolf
Gene Federico
Louis Danziger
Jacques Garamond
Christof Gassner
Alan Fletcher
John Gorham
Rudolf deHarak
Takenobu Igarashi
Roger Law
Les Mason
Shin Matsunaga
Armin Hofmann
Wolfgang Weingart
Henry Steiner
Shigeo Fukuda
Helmut Schmid
Paula Scher
Shigeo Fukuda
Benno Wissing
Alan Fletcher
Bruno Monguzzi

Transforming the ordinary

Strathmore, **Massachusetts, 1989**

Strathmore What makes Saul Bass tick? If you hadn't been a designer, what might you have been?

Bass I was either an archaeologist in my last incarnation, or I will be one in my next life, because I have a passionate interest in archaeology.

Strathmore For a person concerned with contemporary culture, as you are, this interest in the past is particularly curious. Where does it come from?

Bass I'm not just interested in the past, but in the very, very, very distant past. What fascinates me is the mystery and unreality of it all. The most intriguing culture is one about which we know a good deal, but not everything. That leaves holes which can be filled with our own fantasies and imagination.

Strathmore Is that why you collect fragments of ancient civilization?

Bass Yes. These objects, in addition to their intrinsic beauty, bring with them a special kind of mystery – a quality of the unknown that reaches a very deep and hidden place.

Strathmore What are your other passions?

Bass Family, friends, simple foods.

Strathmore Simple foods?

Bass I like foods that are normally nondescript, when they are done extraordinarily. Like soup. A good soup, good fresh bread. They make my soul sing.

Strathmore Is there a connection between that point of view and your view of design?

Bass Yes. And film too. It's the notion of taking a "known," even a cliché and treating it in such a way as to cause it to become an entirely fresh experience. Sort of transforming the ordinary into the extraordinary.

Strathmore How do you approach a new design project?

Bass A client comes to you with a definition of the problem, or ideas about what they want to accomplish. Sometimes they have a sophisticated view of it, sometimes they don't. I find myself frequently spending time with the client redefining the problem, backing up, going back to the beginning. Not infrequently the "problem" turns out to be a "symptom". You have to sometimes

5

move back in order to move forward, to really understand what the nature of the solution should be.

Strathmore And once you understand its nature, how do you translate it to design?

Bass My intent with graphic work is almost always to find a visual phrase which is more than it at first seems, or in some way different than it first seems.

Strathmore What are the means?

Bass Ambiguity and metaphor are often central to my work, and certainly to the work of most of the filmmakers and designers I admire.

My predilection for indirection is as much practical as it is aesthetic. Things that are what they appear to be make their point and soon grow tiresome. The ambiguous is intrinsically more interesting, more challenging, more involving, more mysterious and more potent. It forces re-examination, adds tension, gives it life. And because there is more to be discovered, has greater longevity.

Strathmore Can ambiguity be taken too far?

Bass Degree of ambiguity is very significant. And it varies both in terms of how appropriate it is for certain kinds of communications, and how necessary it is for others. Of course, under some circumstances you find yourself skirting the edge of obscurantism. And conversely, a timid use of metaphor puts you in risk of boredom. I suppose there's nothing worse than boredom.

Strathmore Do you still find it a challenge?

Bass My greatest challenge is satisfying my own expectations. I'm a much tougher critic of my own output than any client I've yet encountered. In general, I tend to escalate my creative ambitions for the project. It increases the risk. It makes it more dangerous, but it keeps everything alive. The potential for failure keeps you very alert.

Strathmore What bit of advice would you give a young designer just out of school?

Bass One of the difficulties that students and young designers have to deal with is a perceptual issue. They look at the exceptional work that's being done. What they see is the end product.

They are not privy to process. They may have the illusion that these things really spring full-blown out of the head of some designer. This is a very unsettling perception for young people, because they struggle with their work. They have a go at it...They redo... It gets better... It slips... It gets worse... It comes back... It comes together.

And maybe it's something that's pretty good, even excellent. But they say to themselves, "Gee, it comes hard and it's so difficult. Am I really suited for this?"

Strathmore But what makes them think it's easy for others?

Bass There are certain characteristics in the work they admire, that

Man with the Golden Arm, film poster for Otto Preminger, 1955

Poster for the Olympic Games
held in Los Angeles, 1984

feed this point of view. One is that a really good solution looks
"inevitable". The other is that in the doing, the designer frequently
has very carefully papered over all the edges and all the cracks.
It may have developed, for instance, as a series of discreet pieces;
elements and ideas have been pushed together, squeezed and
compressed, and painted and lacquered and sanded, and what you
have is this beautiful, impervious, monolithic, glowing sphere,
which looks like it emerged in that pristine state in the moment
of birth. The fact of the matter is that everybody works at it.
Works very hard at it. And process, for the experienced designers,
is the same as process for beginning designers. Everybody's working
in the quarry. The only difference is, the experienced designer has
been around awhile and has an experiential track record. There's
less anxiety about the process because you know eventually you're
going to get there. You're also a little more sinewy. You've been
working out a little more. But the process is the same.

Also designers tend to feed those misperceptions. They say
things like "Well, I was in a restaurant and I scribbled it on the
napkin..." or "I was shaving...", "I was on the plane...", "I was in
the taxi..." or whatever. It's not malevolent. It's just that they really
would like to believe that's the way it happened. It's a comfort
to us to think that it could happen that way. And sometimes it does.
But usually it doesn't. So, the good news for students is, we're all
in the same boat. We're all experiencing the same thing. The bad
news is, it isn't going to get any better. So hang in!

Strathmore How do you keep it all in perspective?

Bass We have to be very careful in looking at what we do and not
pump it up. It's useful and interesting, it's fun, it's entertaining,
it livens up our environment, livens up our lives.

And while it can occasionally provide an insight about ourselves
or our culture, it doesn't make a profound contribution to humanity.
Our absorption in what we do tempts us to enlarge the societal
values we ascribe to our activity. We have a role. A modest role.
And, of course, we want to play that out as best we can. What is,
however, really important about design is that it makes many of
us feel good, and it happens to be our lives!

PIETER BRATTINGA

Netherlands

Heroes

Print, New York, November/December 1991

If you asked me to cite an individual who has made a particularly significant contribution to design, I could name one but would inmediately think of another and another and another. Then, thinking about your statement "contribution to design", I wouldn't know what kind of design.

Edgar Kaufmann commissioned Frank Lloyd Wright to make "Falling Waters"! Thereby contributing tremendously to design. Walter Paepke changed the image of the Container Corporation of America by commissioning Herbert Bayer. Wil Sandberg, a typographer, designed all the catalogues and invitations for his own Stedelijk Museum. Adriano Olivetti was a leader in sponsoring architecture, industrial design, graphic design and social awareness.

Except for Sandberg, all the above-mentioned were not designers; in short, it is difficult to evaluate one contribution against another. I do not know if you are aware of the intellectual exchange in pictures and words between Milton Glaser and his client Olivetti. Milton introduced some details in his posters which are references to old Italian masterpieces. The way Milton Glaser did it was over and beyond the strict assignment, thereby creating for the public a significant and humorous contribution to design.

There are "unsung heroes" in design. All those designers working in non-German, -French or -English language areas. They never got the chance to have their work written up. Think of all the discoveries we have made during the last ten years in regard to those tremendous experiments of the 1920s. Slowly we are discovering vast sources of inspiration which we did not know because the material was in Russian, Polish or whatever.

As for my own design, I had the feeling that while I was not always as creative as my "elders", I was better at visual translation and getting the message across in a shorter and cheaper way, though maintaining a high level of sophistication and mystique.

Sandberg, from 'Experimenta Typografica', 1956

Pieter Brattinga

P ieter is ubiquitous. I've encountered him in streets and cafés in Amsterdam, book shops in Soho, Gargonza village in Tuscany, sushi bars in Tokyo, his house in Kootwijk, at Pentagram in London and at conferences everywhere. Like a medieval mason he trades his talents and philosophy around the world.

Pieter is entrepreneurial. Who else would call his commercial design office "Form Mediation", have graphic design exhibitions in a printing works, produce *Quadrat* – an esoteric publication on miscellaneous oddities, open a gallery in a corridor in Amsterdam, present his secretary with a revealing photograph of his heart operation, write an incomprehensible book on design planning and a literate treatise on Sandberg. He may not be a polymath or a Renaissance man, but he does a lot of things.

Pieter is an encyclopaedic resource, a coherent and eloquent talker, a demanding teacher, a challenging colleague. He's generous with his time, an enthusiastic organizer and, I suspect, a shrewd man of business. I'm told he can be a moody son of a bitch, but there's no doubt he's made a lot of waves and influenced a generation of students.

Pieter is elegant. He wears bespoke Mao suits, collects kokeshi dolls, lives in style, has an insouciant air, and an intellectual turn of mind. His lady is a pianist – a good-looker. He has a perceptive wit, a sharp tongue, and is a pleasure over a convivial supper.

By the way, Pieter is also a terrific designer!

Pieter Brattinga

HENRY WOLF

USA

Alexey Brodovitch

**Address: Accepting the "Hall of Fame" award on behalf of Brodovitch,
New York Art Directors Club, September 1972**

Alexey Brodovitch only wore one kind of suit. It was grey, rumpled and one size too large. It seemed that just sitting there, all three buttons buttoned, his hands awkwardly clutching a pencil, a Martini or the Picayune cigarettes he was fond of, just sitting there was agony. Only his eyes were loose, observing, editing, clarifying. His voice came almost as a footnote, an afterthought, a stage whisper with a heavy Russian accent. During the winter of '48 when I first met him, he was teaching at the New School, and had broken his leg; or had it broken by being run over, by the only truck whose owner he couldn't sue because they were also his employers, the Hearst Corp. Some of the students who were eager to know him better had a beer with him after class. The truth was that you never got to know him any better than the very first time. And it was this mystery, this vacuum that he created that was the big force that generated a desire to please, to help him, to relieve his discomfort by bringing him, like an offering, the best work one was capable of producing.

Oh, of course he was a good designer and superb typographer and had an innate sense of elegance about space. But his layouts were done only as approximations.

He stood in the middle of the room and, with a scissor, cut out photostats which he taped to a piece of paper. Others later straightened them. It was in communicating an idea, a mood, a criticism that he was precise and masterful.

I followed him in his job at *Bazaar* where he had reigned (and I use the word advisedly) for a quarter of a century. I suffered from his excellence for months.

Irving Penn once said in a tribute to Alexey Brodovitch that all designers and photographers, whether they knew it or not, owed him a tremendous debt. We are here tonight to make a small down payment.

10

GENE FEDERICO

USA

BCG The work of Brownjohn, Chermayeff and Geismar

The Liberated Page, ed. Herbert Spencer, London, 1960
(first appeared in *Typographica* 2, December 1960)

The resolution lies manifest in many, if not all graphic problems upon which the designer engages. The degree and quality of his perceptive ability and the selective sense which he is able to apply to a particular problem determine how successfully he finally exposes the form and shape of this resolution. Interwoven so as to be an inseparable part of this form and shape are those honest elements and pertinent devices which, although not initially read, sharpen the message with subliminal effect. There are some admirable personal systems of work which produce for the senses food with the fat removed. And when this food is digested by a raptured audience the remembrance is clear and the reaction unconfused. The aware designer's intuitive and acquired knowledge invests in him a more reliable sense of his times and of the needs of the people. Sensing these, he is able to "talk" directly. He *knows* intuitively the language of his day and, whereas research groups may possibly note the effectiveness of his work of yesterday, they cannot even indicate the imperceptible changes from yesterday's "language" to today's, let alone the "language" of tomorrow. It is evident in the work of Brownjohn, Chermayeff and Geismar, that they are well versed in this "language" of today, and they use it with virtuosity. Moreover, there is more than a suggestion that they have already perceived some of tomorrow's "sounds".

From *Watching Words Move,*
an exercise that was originally
self-published

Booklet cover, from the
time when nuclear policy
was hotly debated

LOUIS DANZIGER

USA

Personal statement, 1969

Contemporary Designers, London, Macmillan, 1984

The problem of the graphic designer is quite different from that of the artist who deals essentially in the private image. Because of the public nature of our work, and because our commissions are generally problems of a specific nature, we find that we are continually trying to satisfy the needs of three distinctly different but not necessarily antagonistic criteria. The three are the concerns of the client, the audience and oneself.

We must, if we accept a commission, use our skills and our judgement to achieve our client's objectives. As socially responsible people we try to accomplish these objectives in a positive way. We do this by performing some service for our audience. We provide information, entertainment and aesthetic pleasure.

Most designers will, I believe, agree with the above. It is in the area of self satisfaction where the methods and goals of designers vary. The concerns and approaches which provide satisfaction for me and direct the nature of my work are as follows.

I am concerned with finding an image which is visually strong and aesthetically gratifying yet also so pertinent to the idea that it becomes difficult to separate form from content.

There is a sense of achievement when one can solve a design problem in an elegant way (the word "elegant" is used here in the scientific sense; the accomplishment of a great deal with a minimum of means).

I am concerned with the production of work that demonstrates intelligence. There is continually a search for clarity and depth rather than cleverness.

Although I recognize that the work we do is essentially ephemeral, it is a source of satisfaction to produce work which avoids faddishness and looks fresh for twenty years or longer.

JACQUES GARAMOND

France

Art and graphics

Art and Graphics, eds Willy Rotzler & Jacques Garamond,
Zurich, ABC Verlag, 1983

The graphic artist, in the broadest sense of the term, is above all "an inventor of images", who draws on his own inner impulses and tries to communicate them through a language of information and gesture. His vocabulary, drawn from the sources of an environment in constant evolution-revolution and stored in the memory in the mysteries of the unconscious, is thrown up randomly in response to external needs and in the emotional forms of his imaginary world.

Faced with the many problems of commercial promotion, he is necessarily subject to a game in which his own sensitivity has to stand aside most of the time in deference to the sales motive for which he is commissioned: the criteria of direct communication, profitability and effectiveness with regard to a very diverse public, will have to be priorities, without forgetting that the signifying image he proposes must be new and surprising.

The many aesthetic currents characterizing our time, the many trends which coincide or collide in the fields of art – architecture, sculpture, painting, music, cinema – this wealth of diverse values creates a spiritual climate that strictly conditions the creators of so-called "applied" arts. This does not have to be demonstrated; the influence of Toulouse-Lautrec and Fernand Léger, Georges Braque and Picasso, among others, on all forms of expression (the poster in particular) is still present in the media today.

Conversely, as in a "game of mirrors", the use of specific advertising elements serves as supports and pretexts to proclaim a re-invented pictorial expression (Warhol, Rotella, Schwitters, Wesselmann and others). Already, in 1916-17, Marcel Duchamp had put up the "Apolinère Enameled" hoarding with the intention of an ambiguous object-subject relationship.

Consequently, that free art has countless influences on and interferences in the overall production of specialist graphic artists is undeniable. Who would question this?

Personally, I can but recognize everything this immense capital has been able to give me in interests: first as an attentive and passionate pupil, then as a novice and finally as a professional in contact with disconcerting realities; art and trade forming a couple

13

Poster for photography
exhibition, "Expofot 1986"

in a perpetual state of divorce that I am always trying to reconcile with varying degrees of happiness. My graphic works will, at least, testify to my hope and my obstinacy to this end.

These commercial works provide a well-defined communication and, if there is a "message", it is mainly that of the client or organization ordering the shaping, the "signalling" of its sales arguments, prestige, or simple information. But the importance of their circulation, the proliferation of advertising sites and their impact on the public give them a value as examples with which I am necessarily involved; a responsibility which is situated precisely at that meeting point where the need for purely personal expression is superimposed over external constraints.

It is this need that directs me towards a diversified field of many activities: painting, drawing, engraving, through which I continue, in relative freedom, the search for a sensitive quality, while choosing to ignore an illusory hierarchy between the various art forms.

CHRISTOF GASSNER

Germany

Designers go the distance:
an exchange of letters with
Victor Malsy

The ecology of form and content, Mainz, Verlag Hermann Schmidt, 1994

The following letters or "short pieces" were always intended for publication. They are designed to turn the spotlight onto Christof Gassner, to show and articulate what was produced before, during and after the work he did for the magazine *Öko-Test.*

3rd July 1994

Dear Christof Gassner,
"When I hear someone like April Greiman commending the new wave to 'people with a healthy visual appetite,' I'd like to reply by saying thanks, I've already eaten." Thus the comment of Helmut Schmid in a letter to Wolfgang Weingart on the new wave from the USA which, in the 1980s, started spilling over into Germany with its lifestyle magazines.
    Thinking back to that period, *Öko-Test-Magazin* stood like a lone lighthouse in those early days of verbal and visual pollution. Its editors and publishers created a publication with actual content, high journalistic standards, and a distinct visual image all of its own. This was sheer madness in the 1980s when anything and everything "new wavy" – the fare the majority lusted after – was being tossed onto the magazine market. At a time such as this, they launch a magazine for a minority, cannot really tell whether the environmental movement with its "muesli design" will even accept it. As if that wasn't enough, they start the project without any financial backing, praiseworthy for some, naïve for others, Herr Gassner, where did you get so much idealism? and the strength, perseverance and energy you needed to survive such a project? But let me correct myself, it was an attitude, an attitude towards social conditions, and towards design, and I bet you still stand by that attitude today, don't you?
Sincerely,
Victor Malsy
10th July 1994

15

Dear Victor Malsy,

Well, I wouldn't like to find myself quite that high up on the pedestal of idealism. There are other reasons I got involved in the Öko-Test project (which, incidentally – I have to correct you here – would not have been possible without any sort of financial backing. By 1990 some 2000 partners had pumped in a total of three million marks), other, more mundane reasons. Curiosity, for example, and a spirit of adventure. What especially appealed to me was the chance to use the freedom it offered me, and to design a magazine counter to the paradigms of the age, the "madness", as you term it, of designing the magazine from its actual contents, publishing a consumer magazine that takes its audience seriously precisely because it does not slavishly tailor its layout to suit their so-called taste but attempts to set more authentic standards.

As such, I pretty much fell between all magazine design stools of the 1980s, between expectations of lifestyle and muesli design. This is reflected in the intense debate over our layout in the readers' letters column. What got them, the readers wrote, was the outer appearance, which not only failed to stand out in any way on newsstand counters but was also completely unattractive in itself, that the sensational presentation made them gag and shudder; why, they asked, did we waste our nice grey paper on cover pages and photos on every single test and report; but then there were some, virtually bowled over by the magazine's layout, who said that reading it was fun.

The fact that I stuck it out so long, despite the animosity and rows (which I sometimes rather enjoyed), is perhaps due to the attitude to design you refer to. I am very dogged, a distance man rather than a sprinter, and like to finish things once I've embarked on them. The problem with magazines, however, is that you can never bring anything to a conclusion, and you resolve each month to design the ultimate, absolute, most appealing issue, but by the middle of the following month you are already resigned, in the face of normal setbacks, and to simply try to get everything to the printers in fairly decent shape. "But next month..." that's what makes it so hard to stop.

In somewhat reproachful fashion, Jurgen Rauschel put my attitude to design in a nutshell: only as graphic artist am I a fundamentalist. In eco-political terms, however, a wimpy "realo".
Sincerely,
Christof Gassner.

14th July 1994

Dear Christof Gassner,
Well, yes, that's also the word on Gassner among colleagues: Gassner is a quiet, retiring, yet dogged apologist of our trade, occasionally a bit of a tough cookie, still, I ask myself whether "graphic fundamentalist" is an accurate description of your position on design. The term has rather negative connotations: black-and-

Following the Chernobyl disaster, I used a quote from the Bible: "MENE; God hath numbered thy kingdom, and finished it. TEKEL; Thou art weighed in the balances, and art found waiting. PERES; Thy kingdom is divided, and given to the Medes and Persians."

white thinking, he projects his narrow view of the world on things because he's scared of change, stubbornly sticking to principles once they're established, come what may.

I don't think you have such a blinkered view of things, for your design oozes a willingness to experiment, in your approach to language and its visual translation, for example. Herr Gassner, who taught you to read, and who focused your vision? Your Zurich teacher Josef Müller-Brockmann was undoubtedly an important figure, yet there must have been other figures in your design career, from the "baumaschinen ag Zurich" in 1962 to the "Kieler Woche" in 1993, what awesome – or awful – figures did you run into?

Your advertising design for "baumaschinen ag Zurich" suggests to me images and names from concrete poetry. I think of Heissenbüttel, Mon, Gomringer, Gappmayr, and the watchword of the concretes: economy of information. To this economy of information – the copy reads like concrete poetry – you add an economy in the visual translation: one typeface, one type size, the line breaks ragged left according to content, and for the interplay of text and image a programme is designed (one can't, of course talk about say "designing a programme" without mentioning the name Karl Gerstner). The means of expression are reduced, word, text and image have not been interfered with in the sense of being unfamiliarized, cut up or montaged, words and letters are virtually "untampered with" in terms of form – virtually, because you do intervene: you write everything lowercase. (Was that the reason the client rejected the designs?)

In the *Öko-Test* "Genetic Engineering" issue, you go a few steps further. Your play instinct leads to ever new combinations of language and characters, familiar words are chopped up, sequences of combinations and sounds find their form in letters and characters: "Al", "fa", "Zu", "bet", "Kunft", "Algenfatechzugie", "Fallaktor", "Hurtschaft". From "Genes admonish Greens" you extract a "no". Breaking words down into their component elements, cutting up letters, you question parts of language that seem to have come to be taken for granted and often lack any real substance. The letters display their form and are taken at their word, and your sixty variations on the word "TEST", the "North-South" poster, the work for "Schauspiele in Fernsehen" ("Theatre on TV") and "Fernseh-Kultur-Programme" ("TV arts programmes") should also be mentioned here.

Reading letters, getting to the bottom of words: this shaping with and in language, understood as speaking, is like a red thread running through your work.
Sincerely,
Victor Malsy
18th July 1994

Dear Victor Malsy,

One immediate response: basically, I am, of course, not a graphic fundamentalist − only, and that's what the quote referred to, I had to assume this guise in the Öko-Test project. One of the odd things I experienced while there was that a lot of people on the left start, once they have got off on the rightist marketing trip in a big way, to internalize the real and supposed market necessities in such a way that you can be left utterly speechless.

But on now to the role models, the awesome − or awful − figures you spoke of. Let's take the latter first: They're everywhere, "A torrent of visual junk information makes our eyes sick and our souls lonely," writes Gottfried Honegger in his foreword to the book Grafik-Design by Odermatt & Tissi, and calls for an "Ökologie der Ästhetik" ("ecology of aesthetics").

The name Gottfried Honegger takes me back to Zurich, to my time as a student. While I was studying at the Kunstgewerbeschule I encountered two quite opposite teachers: Josef Müller-Brockmann and Walter Käch. Müller-Brockmann's position as an unrelenting exponent of the "Neue Grafik" is well documented, his traffic and music posters are landmarks in the history of poster design, and the entire graphic arts class succumbed to his charismatic influence in the years he taught in Zurich (1957–60). Walter Käch is probably less present in people's minds. A pioneer of Swiss graphic art in the 1920s and 1930s, he subsequently devoted himself principally to the study of Roman capitals. He acted as an antithesis whose significance I only became aware of much later. While Müller-Brockmann taught the "anonymity and functionalism of design elements, which find their equivalent in the geometric form of design (and there only)" and "willingly submit to the elements system," Käch demanded "rhythm and proportions as a law in nature and in typography" and presented what was for him "the shaping geometry, the formative law of a lifeless material." While the Müller-Brockmann class worked exclusively with a single face (Akzidenz Grotesk, what else?), Walter Käch, when asked which sans serif grotesk he considered the ideal form, replied "there's no way a sans serif grotesk could even be called 'ideal'."

About the same time in Basle, the first work of the Gerstner & Kutter atelier was appearing. Though the formal vocabulary was very familiar to me, their approach to it was very different. Signs became modifiable (the "boîte à musique" logo), the simple, clear Swiss screen was turned into a complex modular system, an encoded typographic programme (the novel "Schiff nach Europa"), in the severe Swiss graphic arts scene plays on language and even comic-like elements began to occur (advertisements for the Rheinbrucke department store); I was simply confused by so much fun: wasn't graphic arts a serious, a deadly serious business? Almost in spite of myself, I admired this work by Gerstner & Kutter very much. (Much more than afterwards, without wishing to disregard their qualities, the much lauded campaigns by the GGK agency.)

Later, in the 1970s, the work of Herb Lubalin, notably the first years of typography magazine U&lc (Upper and lower case) broadened my

horizons. Lubalin did simply everything a well brought-up typographer from Switzerland (or Ulm) doesn't do: centre axis – hadn't we overcome this relic from the Renaissance? Monumental uppercase texts – hadn't this been exposed as typography of the ruling classes? Didn't all these ligatures, symbioses and metamorphoses, these textures and calligraphies, initials and vignettes belong on the scrap heap of typo-history? As if that wasn't enough, Herb Lubalin also kept quoting, in word and image, directly and indirectly, the salons of the belle époque, *and the cancellareschi of the Italian Renaissance, the graffiti of the New York subway and, equally, the inscriptions of the Romans, the Irish writers of the eighth century, or the anonymous typesetters in the Wilhelmine (late nineteenth/early twentieth century) period, etc. Yet the most astounding thing was: in Lubalin's U&lc, this all became new and lively, incredibly present, never seemed archaic or historicizing but always excitingly up-to-date. Many defenders of the typographic faith doubtless view things differently; for me, Herb Lubalin remains a major and exciting stimulus.*
Sincerely,
Christof Gassner

22nd July 1994

Dear Christof Gassner,
Müller-Brockmann, Käch, Gerstner, Lubalin: more divergent figures cannot be encountered in our design career, and I guess only a tough cookie such as you could come out of it all unscathed. When I first read the name Lubalin, my hair stood on end. I suppose I am something of a defender of the faith myself. For me, Lubalin is an excitable boy for whom, in the land of boundless possibilities, everything seemed possible.

Yet on now to another point in your most recent letter. You write that "a lot of people on the left start, once they have got off on the rightist marketing trip in a big way, to internalize the real and supposed market necessities in such a way that you can be left utterly speechless." What does that mean? Did the alternative *Öko-Test* project, with its quite specific make-up, change the way many a left head thought in the sense that designed media (from letterheads via posters to magazines) may indeed have something to do with the actual content? Or do heads such as these also use design primarily as a form of surface cosmetics?
Sincerely,
Victor Malsy

In the other issues, the interplay of different topics was the featured topic, producing a series of typographic 'cover programmes'

The leaf in the logo is turned into the cover motif: 'cover leaf' and 'cover sheet' in one.

25th July 1994

Dear Victor Malsy,
No, I don't believe that, except in a few rare instances, there is much interest in media design in the "Green alternative" scene. True it has moved away from the homespun, the muesli design – I fear, however, in the wrong direction. Be it for the Bündnis 90/Greens election posters, Greenpeace-Magazin or Journal, or Öko-Test itself, it's not autonomous designs we want but design based on poll and ratings – everything today's media market demands, in other words.
I sometimes ask myself whether my way of designing magazines isn't fast coming to its sell-by date. But then, yesterday, I saw Tatjana, the new film by Aki Kaurismäki, which really is classic Kaurismäki, as Die Zeit, wrote. Absolutely stunning! So stuff such as this is still being produced after all.
Sincerely,
Christof Gassner
P.S. As for Lubalin, whether he's "exciting" or just an "excitable boy", shall we agree to disagree, or agree on the following: live wire that he is, he's certainly very "citable".

9th August 1994

Dear Christof Gassner,
"For the optimist, life isn't a problem but itself already the solution." Marcel Pagnol.
I consider myself one of the boundless optimists, admit that I sometimes read the world in this sense, as I do your phrase that the way you design magazines is coming up to its sell-by date: let's say your approach is coming up to its sail-by date, is about to leave the shelter of its harbour and embark on a long journey. You, Christof Gassner, carry hope within you, so what new model is currently on the keel-blocks?
Since 1986, you have been professor of design and typography, first in Darmstadt and, since 1992, in Kassel. This must demand a lot of confidence and hope. Try as I may, however, I can't picture you as a dogged apologist expounding *ex cathedra* recipes for successful design, far less as one who teaches a style, a pattern which, when correctly applied, will garner a design, communication or typography award. How do you see yourself as teacher? How do you view orientation for students of our subject? Many teachers see the job of providing orientation as a categorical imperative, preaching rules and studiously ignoring the fact that many of the facts are nothing but their own opinion, their own "good taste".
Almost twenty years ago, Peter Von Kornatzki described the then state of typography as follows: "Though it (typography) is less

a utilitarian art than ever before, its utilitarian value is very highly rated. Typography is alive! It might not think itself as important as it did ten or twenty years ago, sees itself less as image, taking a backseat to the actual text. Despite this, however, it is an important part of "visual communication".

Hasn't this situation since changed fundamentally? The typography of recent years has advanced to become a utilitarian art, and its utilitarian value is, in many places, measured in the awards and recognition it is given. For many a designer, contests have become the real clients and are the measure of successful design. Today's typography thinks itself more important than ever before, and its function – communicating visually – is ever more frequently subservient to its entertainment value. Ever since design mutated into an "economic factor", firms, too, have been merrily joining in this entertainment act.

Sincerely,

Victor Malsy

P.S. Regarding our Lubalin "business"; yes, he is very "citable", a judgement worthy of Solomon.

16th August 1994

Dear Victor Malsy,
You certainly stood my "sell-by date" on its head – in a manner both artful and kind. Up until now, it's only been instances of words and phrases twisted in the opposite direction that have stuck in my mind, such as André Heller's "giving up a letter", or an interesting "insider" phrase used at ZDF television, when something wasn't correctly underlaid, a line incorrectly spaced for example: "that will broadcast itself out."

A few comments – more isn't possible in this context – on my teaching work: I have no recipes or patterns, and certainly none likely to produce quick successes. Perhaps, however, I did (and do) sometimes manage to convey something of the fun designing can be if it is pursued seriously, with intensity, that is, with passion, with obsession. One point of departure is a very elementary basics type course, with lots of handcraft, lots of experimenting with simple forms. This is no big new insight, of course, but more necessary than ever before; otherwise, with ever more PC user interfaces, I would soon find myself in the role of the professor in Eugène Ionesco's Lesson, whose student can quickly calculate "three billion seven hundred and fifty million nine hundred and ninety thousand two hundred and fifty-one times five billion one hundred and sixty-two million three hundred and three thousand five hundred and eight," yet is unable to answer the question, "What is four take away three?": "Four take away three is... four?.. Well, three then... Or could it perhaps be ten?"

A further point: leading the way to a typographic shaping of use and understanding (as opposed to one of consumption) calls for intense concern with contents: only from this, I feel, can truly innovative typographic formulations issue, only from this a form of design which really does communicate visually, which makes a statement, design that does not decoratively paste over or obscure contents in such a way that no contents worth speaking of are left.

Important to me too is memory. We're currently running a magazine project in Kassel on the history of lettering and typography: UberSchrift. One of my aims is to show that typographic design did not begin with the dawn of the modern age or with El Lissitzky. Many of the basic text/image patterns in modern magazine design, to stick with the subject under discussion, can be found in the Schedelschen Weltchronik published in 1493 by Nuremberg printer Anton Koberger or, to go back further, in the thirteeth-century Falconry Book of Frederick II. The winner of the 1980 Nobel Prize for Literature, Czeslaw Milosz, spoke of the "age that refuses to remember". For me, this judgement is reflected in many of the new typo trends of the 1980s, in new wave, punk and the post-modern, which again remind me of typography between 1850 and 1890: it, too, was very pleasant and is still popular with collectors at flea markets.

I don't want to let the Marcel Pagnol quote go unanswered: "There is a chain connecting all events in this best of all possible worlds; for if you had not been booted out of a beautiful mansion for the love of Lady Cunegonde, and if you had not tangled with the Inquisition, and had not wandered across America on foot, and had not struck the Baron with your sword, and lost all those sheep you brought from Eldorado, you would not be here eating candied citrons and pistachios." Voltaire, Candide.
Sincerely,
Christof Gassner

22

ALAN FLETCHER

UK

John Gorham

Le Arti, Italy, 1976

W ith John Gorham alphabets are pictogramic and words illustrations. Unencumbered by formal visual education, he served his apprenticeship on the treadmill of commercial advertising. His spiritual portfolio is a cornucopia of fresh ideas, unlimited curiosity, unbounded enthusiasms, inventive forms and pleasurable solutions. His pictorial communications avoid intellectual pretension, his inclinations to nostalgia are tempered by originality of thought, he owes less to the typographic niceties and formal canons postulated by classic type designers than the stimulus of personal observations. He often borrows from the naiveté of fairground calligraphy, the energy of early advertising, the uninhibited vigour of jobbing printing. The charm of printed ephemera: candy wrappers, comic papers, shop façades, the folk art of cigarette cards.

JOHN GORHAM

UK

What I think about graphic design

Idea, European designers issue, Japan, 1969

Idea Magazine have asked me to write an article on what I think about graphic art and its future. This I find very hard as I haven't any real philosophy on the subject, but I will do my best to say some of the things I find important to my work. The most difficult thing I am finding at the moment is to stay small. I have no aspirations towards becoming a large company (or even a small one), because I feel it means you have to become a businessman first and a designer second. I have spoken to different design organizations and they all say the same thing: "When you start to expand your troubles begin." This usually means your work suffers and I am not prepared for this to happen to me. The kind of work I do is very personal to me and I like to have complete control over it. Because of that I not only like to do the design but also execute the artwork myself.

I don't have, nor do I want, a particular style. I feel the most important thing is to come up with an idea first, then invent a style from that. Each job I tackle really terrifies me. I am always trying to invent something different. The trouble with this is you need time to experiment and unfortunately most jobs are wanted quickly. This does mean that jobs do occasionally go wrong as there just isn't enough time left to develop the idea properly. However, I prefer it to be this way as I get bored repeating myself more than once. I would rather risk a cock-up every now and again than have the same look to every job.

I have found the real trouble begins when you do something new, such as giving lettering a fresh look, because then everyone expects you to do that when they give you a job. Very often the job doesn't require lettering but a completely different approach. I find a lot of art directors are more concerned with the superficial look of a job instead of looking deeper into the problem and trying to find out what it is supposed to say. On many occasions I have been asked to do a piece of "John Gorham-type lettering" as though I was some kind of mindless machine.

Something I have tried very hard to avoid is over-exposure, as I am sure in the long run it proves ruinous. You might think this rather contradictory considering the business we are in and that my

Logo for a part-work series,
Time-Life International, 1971

Heading for an article in
Harpers Bazaar, 1969

Motion picture logo for the
Rank Organization, 1975

work is appearing in this book, but I don't mean avoid all publicity, obviously a little from time to time can be a great help. What I really mean is not to have your work seen in all the advertising agencies and in all the magazines you can get in. Everyone then feels they know what you are doing and this leads to your becoming stale quickly. I believe in keeping them guessing. I don't think anyone really knows what I will come up with next (including myself!).

In my early days I used to get my stimulation from other designers, i.e. Alan Fletcher, Bob Gill, Pushpin, Herb Lubalin and others, but in reality what I was doing was an imitation of them. During the past couple of years, though, I have found less and less excitement at looking at other designers' work and more excitement in things around me in everyday life such as shops, pubs, funfairs, suburban life. These things have a fresh quality to them because they have a free expression of their own. The sadness is that all the things I have mentioned are being changed by graphic designers who, more often than not, take all the life out of the subject and replace it with a rigid, dead look. One of the deadest things nowadays is the styling for brewery houses. Recently I visited the North of England and on the way I passed pub after pub with the same boring look instead of the beautiful individuality they used to have. And it doesn't stop there, it seems as though most companies want this uniform look created for them. Fortunately the new young designers of England are reacting against this and their work has a feeling for the environment in which they live.

I am not sure what the future holds for me as I haven't any clearly defined direction. There are areas still left to explore, such as television and films, but I can't see this happening for some time. What I usually find is that every so often something comes along which offers me a new challenge and which in turn directs my course for a while.

RUDOLPH deHARAK

USA

Thoughts on Modernism

AIGA Journal of Graphic Design, vol.5, no.2, 1987

In the late 1940s as a beginning commercial artist in Los Angeles, I attended two lectures which introduced me to Modernism and had a profound effect on my life. The first was a lecture by Will Burtin entitled "Integration, The New Discipline in Design". Burtin not only spoke about design and communications, but also presented an exhibition of his work, which guided the viewer through a series of experiences which were described as the four principal realities of visual communications. They were the reality of man, as measure and measurer; the reality of light, colour, and texture; the reality of space, motion, and time; and reality of science. He was the first person I had heard use the term "visual communications".

A short time later, I heard Gyorgy Kepes speak. At the time I didn't fully understand everything he was saying, yet I knew that his words were very important to me. I recall my excitement, as I was able to draw parallels between what he was saying about the plastic arts and what Will Burtin had said concerning the realities of visual communications.

It was the beginning of my realization that it was possible to communicate visual information which transcended common conventions and could become art. I discovered the possibility of having a viable vocation and at the same time to be able to experience deep fulfilment. These lectures were so important that they inspired me to leave my job as a mechanical artist and commit myself totally to design.

As I became more involved with this profession, I realized that my deepest concerns with design were centered on what I felt were the mysteries of form – discovering new forms and using them to construct creative and meaningful solutions to design problems.

I attempted to evolve forms that covered the entire emotional spectrum and were also impeccable in their sense of order. This to me was the essence of Modernism, and toward that end, I wanted to create constellations so rich that they could communicate content. I was searching for what I called "the hidden order"; trying to find some common principle or scheme inherent in all things that would answer questions that maybe I hadn't yet asked.

Armin Hofmann: trademark for the Swiss National Exhibition, Expo 1964

Odermatt & Tissi: trademark for weavers and textile printers, Mettler + Co., 1969

Rudolf deHarak: trademark for the Kurt Versen Lighting Company, 1957

The Bauhaus was perhaps the most profound example of Modernism in their break with the rigid ideologies of "grand manner" art education. Dedicated to research and instruction, their objective was a social reconditioning through a synthesized curriculum. Simultaneously, all of the arts were examined in the light of contemporary conditions.

Modernism is also exemplified in the International Style of design that developed following World War II. Its mostly Swiss contributors included such notable designers as Max Bill, Josef Müller-Brockman, Armin Hofmann, Max Huber, Richard Lohse, Hans Neuberg, Siegfried Odermatt, Emil Ruder, and Carlo Vivarelli. These Modernists breathed new life into design, cutting away all unnecessary graphic appendages and leaving only the essentials. Their work was thoughtful and systematic. It was beautiful, thoroughly crafted, and communicated complex information quickly and simply.

In the 1940s and 1950s, I believed that Modern design was a means to precipitate reactions and new actions. At that time, there was a sense of urgency – a design revolution that was alive, that aimed at developing openness to what many considered radical forms of communication. The goal was to create a platform for design from which could be communicated bold, new graphic ideas. I think that platform today is firmly rooted, thus expanding the possibility of producing intensely creative, dynamic and even bizarre ideas. There is now much more awareness and acceptance of good design.

As times changed, so did my design philosophies. Now I am more interested in the process of problem-solving. This is not to say I don't want my design to be beautiful. But in the past I was preoccupied with finding something profound and revealing within a form. Today I am much more concerned with the clear, direct communication of an idea.

Twenty-five years ago I said in a lecture, "The attitudes that forms communicate dictate the ultimate validity of a design. Form is necessary and vital to the expression of ideas. Without it, content is barren. So in an effort to effect a solution to any visual problem, the designer relies on his abilities to create new forms or use existing forms in unique concepts, and manipulate them."

Just a few years ago at another lecture I made quite a different statement. "Design is a problem-solving process, but for many of us it is much more than that. It is also a very personal process of searching for and developing new concepts that serve to clarify and extend ideas. Herein lies the creativity in design.

"The climate that the designer works within is very complex, and as in all creative fields, at times painful and frustrating. The designer's work must satisfy the tastes and opinions of the client, but most important, it must successfully reach and communicate to the audiences for which the work is intended. Even though the design

27

work should also be self-rewarding, it is frequent that personal preferences have little meaning in the solving of design problems."

The differences in these two statements, made more than twenty years apart, are apparent. Yet, because my fundamental belief in Modernism has not changed, I believe that they mostly represent a shift in emphasis and priorities.

Before I became fully aware of the International Style, and the Swiss pioneers in particular, my design inclinations moved in a somewhat similar direction. Before we had Helvetica in the United States, I primarily used sans-serif typefaces such as Futura, News Gothic, and Franklin Gothic. When Helvetica was first introduced, I specified it almost exclusively because it had a purity and uniformity that signaled no-nonsense information without embellishment. It is the way I feel about the old Remington typewriter typeface – beautiful, direct, and systematized. Typography is a profound issue, and when I started in this field, I felt that developing an understanding of all typefaces would be an extraordinary, time-consuming challenge.

It was preferable for me to work with just a few typefaces on a consistent basis, thereby developing a more intimate understanding of the letterforms. The challenge and ideal solution to a book design, for example, could be to set the entire book – titles, subtitles, text and folios – in one style and size, establishing priorities of information through position and spatial relationships.

I am not implying that this approach was better than others, but it gave me a more disciplined position in which to understand type and to achieve viable solutions. Moreover, in designing a record cover on the music of Mozart, I was never interested in using a typeface that would be representative of the eighteenth century. Personally, I can no more identify Mozart with Caslon than with Futura. If I were to follow this design philosophy to its conclusion, it would be logical to put flames on the word "fire" or ice-caps on the word "cool". I believe the problem-solving process requires intelligent selection of a typeface that functions most appropriately for an overall design concept.

Changes in style, or new preferences in typefaces or color, have little to do with the basic responsibilities of problem-solving in visual communications. The designer making a poster today has the same responsibilities to communicate clearly as El Lissitzky, Rodchenko, or Cassandre had decades ago.

I don't believe in change for the sake of change. Change comes about through a natural process of development or because something needs improving. Modernism suggests movement which is ahead of its time. If we do something that has been done before, we are not being creative; we are being redundant. Creativity, which is what Modernism is all about, is a constant searching process that promises a greater chance for failure than it does for success.

TAKENOBU IGARASHI

Japan

My relationship to design

Lecture: Design in economic performance – Japan and Germany compared, Essen, May 1993

Through my eastern eyes I have studied western design, and through my eastern mind I have continued to design. I want to think of design in a free manner, challenging different tasks. Such a challenge fulfils me with great joy. I find it important to apprehend design – whether in the field of graphic, product or three-dimensional design – from the standpoint of daily life and environment, and to practise it within the flow of design history.

The field of design, including education, is much too specialized. Our lives and thoughts are actually of a comprehensive nature. The borders between different design disciplines should be opened. We should be free to examine product design from the viewpoint of graphic design or three-dimensional design, and vice versa. Through this process of interaction, new impulses are gained in creating new design.

Although the importance of team discussion in the design process is indisputable, it is my belief that design decisions should be made individually. The individual feeling for design should be valued, regardless of the results of market research or what the marketing specialist says. The designer must be a strong individual, making independent decisions. I would like to be such a designer, and in order to realize my design ideas, I take the initiative in proposing projects and work with clients who want to realize them.

The typical characteristic of my work is to create a new design-oriented enterprise for the client. My work consists of creating products for the new enterprise and doing all the necessary design – from product, brand identity, developing adequate sales channels up to graphic and display design. Through this new venture, the client develops a new corporate character, which eventually leads to a need for a new corporate identity. My design activity is that of proposing a project and doing the required design.

In the past fifteen years numerous Japanese companies introduced new corporate identity programmes. Among these companies, only a handful of them actively planned to venture into a new market. Most others simply imitated other corporate identities, or introduced them without a long-range plan as a "special event" celebrating an anniversary or a round sum of profits. Most corporate identities are

SUNTORY

Suntory logo, 1990

Suntory chart, 1990

designed by advertising agencies, which in Japan exert stronger influence over their clients than their counterparts in the West. On the average, corporate identity design takes six to twenty-four months to develop. In most cases, corporate identity strategy is considered complete with the application of a new logo. After that point enthusiasm and effort in creating a new corporate image decline rapidly. The power of contemporary Japanese graphic design was never utilized so extensively in terms of scale and planning as a marketing strategy as in the corporate identity movement.

A new corporate identity must have support within the company, and must present a positive image to the outside world. Now, how are design decisions made? At this crucial point, differences become apparent between Japanese and western ways. In Japan the notion of *sho* (pine), *chiku* (bamboo), *bai* (plum) is widely used in every aspect of life. For example, in a Sushi restaurant, *sho-chiku-bai* stands for three menu categories depending on price, with *sho* as the most expensive. In a design presentation, it is necessary to show three ideas which correspond to the notion of *sho-chiku-bai,* with *sho* as the recommended design, and *chiku* and *bai* as alternatives. The second and the third choices are always presented even though it is taken for granted that *sho* will be chosen.

Formal decisions are often made long after the presentation, although all participants at the presentation may have agreed on the design. Compared to clients in the west, Japanese clients take much longer in making final decisions. This is because the one in charge of decision-making at the presentation does not necessarily have the power to make the final decision.

The difference in decision-making between the east and the west has its roots in the difference between image thinking and logical thinking. I also believe that language plays an important role here, in that it affects the left and the right sides of the brain in different ways, affecting the speed of decision-making. Compared to 126 letters of the alphabet, there are 7000 different symbols – *Hiragana, Katakana, Kanji* and Roman letters – used in the Japanese language. The greatest part of which is *Kanji,* the ideographic Chinese writing which is not only numerous but also difficult to differentiate due to various examples of identical pronunciations with different meanings. Thus, verbal communication is often very ambiguous, making exact communication only possible through writing. Maybe that is the reason why Japanese always like to exchange business cards at their first meeting. Moreover, Japanese can be written horizontally and vertically, and even from right to left. Because it is an ideograph made up of units, one can usually guess the meaning and the pronunciation of an unknown *Kanji* character. However, it takes a long time to truly understand the full meaning. Striving to be international, many companies discarded their beautiful

Hibiki sculpture (model),
client Suntory Ltd., 1986

traditional logos and exchanged them for an alphabetical logo design. Perhaps it is the image thinking that made corporate identity introduction so effective in Japan. Every day an average of 400 applications for trademark registration are submitted in Japan, that means 146,000 a year, including brand logos. Today, now that the big corporate identity boom is over, designers must seek a new role in the field of corporate image and corporate communication.

In recent times, corporations have taken up interest in supporting cultural activities. Some have even built concert halls and museums. Similar to the event-oriented Japanese corporate identity programmes, these projects also seem to contain an element of ambiguity.

The deep-rooted Japanese image thinking seems to act positively on creativity. I also believe that ambiguity is very important in design, especially in the future. Ambiguity is often felt at times of decision-making in design, a specific Japanese situation resulting from the complexity of language and image thinking. The world of *aimai* is difficult to translate into other languages. Therefore, we should continue to nurture ambiguity in the realm of creativity, but we should also try to communicate simply and clearly to the rest of the world.

The next move I anticipate in the field of Japanese design is to develop appropriate products suitable to the new faces the companies have taken on. Until now, great efforts have been made to renovate the façade, leaving the content behind. Companies should get back to the roots of business in which they make cultural contributions to society through their products. Ecology is also an important theme. It is necessary to build up an economical system which functions without mass production. On this point we can refer to the countless local traditional manufacturers existing all over Japan. Here we find models for new directions such as natural material, comfortable pace, a virtually unchanging product, and excellent craftsmanship. These small companies have contributed to society for several hundred years in their own ways. What they lack now is the ability to develop new products suitable to the needs of our times and to establish new sales channels.

ROGER LAW

UK

Mondo bizarro

Unpublished, 1995

The topical puppet show *Spitting Image* has so far enjoyed a run of more than a decade on British television. This success has resulted in a vast number of spin-offs from best-selling comedy books to politicians as toby jugs, rubber dog-chews and so on. Some of the notions that never happened are even stranger. I remember a proposal from TV scientist Heinz Wolff involving the puppets in a crazed idea about shooting nuclear waste into space. We passed on that one.

There was also the condom book – your favourite prophylactic politicians caricatured in latex. The book itself was a bellows – as you turned the page up popped "Johnny Major". A prototype was ingeniously designed by my partner Peter Fluck. The publishers Faber and Faber were amazed at the book's ingenuity but the production costs were prohibitive. People will only pay so much for a joke.

Perhaps the most extraordinary aspect of the topical puppet show is its universality. Over the past few years similar shows have sprung up from Moscow to Tokyo and it is this aspect that I find most intriguing.

The first approach was from the West Germans. They arrived at our East End Studios and wanted puppets made for a show they assured us would offend no one and would be in no way satirical. We said we thought those qualities were rather the point and after some debate we sent them back to West Germany to do their own thing. They did and ironically the show they produced, entitled *Gum*, did acquire a cutting edge. I saw a pastiche of the German movie *Das Boot* with the entire German government sitting in a U-Boat that was being depth-charged. It was very effective.

The Italians came next – Paula Messiah, from Global Communications. Spitting Image made puppets of the entire Italian government, sent them to Italy, and the Italian production team wrote and produced the show *Teste di Gomma*. On the day the show was to premier the entire Italian government resigned. Not good news for our Italian colleagues. We rang them up to commiserate only to be told not to worry. The politicians would just re-shuffle and take different jobs – *no problemo*.

Cicciolina
(Italy)

The next arrival was a lone Hungarian, Miklos Salusinsky, who wanted to make a show in Budapest. He had a great deal of determination and no money. I showed him all the processes by which the British show was made and he went back to Budapest and eventually made a very successful Hungarian version on an x-ray of a shoe-string. I visited his Aladdin Film Studios in central Budapest in 1994 and was taken aback by the ingenuity the penniless production team had brought to the show. Miklos had told me over the phone that he had no money for sets but looking at his show reel he had the most extraordinarily elaborate set of the interior of the Hungarian House of Parliament. When I pointed this out he told me that they filmed all of the topicals in the actual House of Parliament. There was some remarkable filming done by balancing the puppeteers on skateboards using a hand-held camera – something we had never tried. The show, *Uborka*, is well-received, mildly satirical and hoping to do better. The producer said to me "You British have been cutting the grass for over 400 years. We Hungarians have only been doing it for four." The show plays all winter and comes off in the summer. I asked him if there was any particular reason for this. He said "Yes – the caricaturist spends the summer in Hösök Tere (the main square) drawing the tourists, where he earns more money."

The Russians. Svetlana Levy is a Tartar by birth and a Tartar by nature. Tall and striking with perfect English, she is utterly autocratic. Svetlana bullied the financial director, Richard Bennett, and myself into travelling to Moscow for a series of meetings with a newly independent production company called "Authors TV" (ATV). We arrived in Moscow during Yeltsin's honeymoon period with the Russian people, though no one seemed to be in control. A Muscovite's idea of capitalism was to stand stock still in lines at the entrances and exits of subways and hotels with two cans of imported lager for sale in one hand and a bedside lamp or some books for sale in the other. The lager would invariably be many months past its sell-by date. On the way to meetings at Ostankino, Moscow's huge TV station, Richard Bennett and I would play "spot the can of lager longest over its sell-by date". We were advised to take showers in the early evening because the whole of Moscow would be watching the newly acquired Mexican soaps on TV, and the water pressure in consequence would be much better at that time.

The Russian producer, Andrei Smirnov, and his colleagues negotiated for several days before a basis for a deal could be put together. We agreed to teach the Russians how to make the puppets and the show. It would be called *Rubber Souls*, a play on the title of Gogol's book *Dead Souls*. In return the Russians agreed to form a company, of which 25 per cent belonged to the British Spitting Image. On our return to London our managing director,

Joanna Beresford, unkindly described the deal as "25 per cent of nothing". Three years later we have yet to prove her wrong. During those years, the Russians have visited the London workshops for training, a visit which culminated in a farewell supper. The British producer, Giles Pilbrow, his director and writers and designer sat down on one side of a long table with their Russian would-be equivalents opposite. The ultimate Indian meal was consumed along with countless bottles of wine, ninety-eight bottles of beer, followed by six bottles of vodka. Speeches were made and tears were shed. The Russian head writer, Sergei Krainev, told an involved joke about a family of worms living on a dung heap, the gist of which was that they had aspirations to live on the dung heap opposite. Not to be left out, one of the British writers told the following joke: "What's the difference between your mother and a terrorist?" No one knew. "You can negotiate with a terrorist." "What do you mean – my mother?" shouted one of the Russians, on the verge of offence. The British writer explained: "Oh gosh, erm, not your mother, any mother, don't you see..." In the end the Russian did see. We toasted the British joke.

At the beginning of last year I received an encouraging fax from Moscow to say that the Rubber Souls team had made a New Year's Eve special, to go out to the nineteen republics from Ostankino. On the night of the broadcast they were told by the TV controller that it was not a good time to laugh at Boris Yeltsin. The New Year's Eve special remained on the shelf.

The first I knew of the Bulgarian satire show, *Coo Coo*, was a phone call from *Private Eye*. Had I time to meet Nelly Andreeva from Bulgaria? Sure – I said. Nelly did not want a franchise – the Bulgarians already had *Coo Coo*, a satire show with one puppet. Nelly had tapes with her and we sat down to watch them. A black news reporter appeared on screen outside the Bulgarian Houses of Parliament. As eminent MPs left the House, the news reporter introduced himself and said he was from Utamba in Africa and asked if they would like to comment on the situation there. Each politician would give a detailed exposition of his party's position on Utamba. The black news reporter then came very close to the camera and confided that he was an exchange student from Zimbabwe and that Utamba did not exist. This routine was followed by a vigorous interview with a military policeman on guard outside a nuclear power station. "Tell me," says the young reporter, "is it true that you have a melt down inside the power station?" The military policeman looked terrified and his denials were none too convincing. This particular item, Nelly told me with a grin, had caused a panic across Bulgaria and Romania – roads blocked with fleeing cars. Rather like the Orson Welles' radio broadcast *War of the Worlds*. Nelly went back to Bulgaria. I thought maybe we should go with her for lessons.

The Greeks came bearing cheques and a deal was struck. I visited the Greeks' studios in the summer of 1994. The studios are in a suburb of Athens in what seems to be an otherwise derelict warehouse sat between a huge olive-oil processing plant (I shall never buy that brand again) and a sluggish slick of evil smelling pollution which could have been a river when Aristotle was a boy. The Greek puppeteers have been drafted from the security guards. They are puppeteers by day and guards by night. The show is, I'm told, 90 per cent political and has very good ratings. The first transmission was hampered by the government calling an election which they lost. The country had a new Socialist government under Andreas Papandreou. Unfortunately, all the puppets were caricatures of the previous administration. Unperturbed, the Greek writers put together a show showing what the previous government would have done had they won the election and stayed in office. No lack of ingenuity in Athens. Mr Ioannis Alafouzos, the owner of the Greek television station Sky, and proprietor of the Greek *Spitting Image* show, is a shipping magnate. I made a number of appointments to meet him, all of which were cancelled. Mr Alafouzos was in court every day fighting the previous government's charges against him for oil smuggling.

Karamanlis
(Greece)

Karel Grelf is a young, energetic entrepreneur from Prague. He arrived at our London studios in 1993 and told me that the first time he saw a tape of a British *Spitting Image* he had promised himself that if the Communist regime crumbled, he would make a similar show in the Czech Republic – and he has. He agreed terms that day and we made arrangements for his team to come to London to be trained. I pointed out that the week he had allocated for his team's visit would coincide with another potential visit by our Russians. Karel roared with laughter and said, "We put up with the Russians for forty years – what's a few more days?" The Russians failed to turn up, but the Czechs arrived. Karel invited me to Prague just before Christmas 1994.

Prague is breathtakingly beautiful in the snow. Ornate and atmospheric, a Christmas pudding of gothic delights. At first glance the city's main obsessions seem to be music, puppets and art, in that order. It seemed very odd to be selling the puppets to the Czechs. Prague has puppet theatres on almost every street corner.

Vaclav Havel
(Czech Republic)

The Czech show, *Gumaci*, is made in an old cinema in the gypsy quarter of Prague. It is put together by a very small team of hard-working professionals. They occasionally get a call from Mr Havel's new friends in Prague castle pointing out that it's not a good idea to portray him as stupid because he most decidedly is not. Their puppet show is well shot, imaginatively lit, and although I can't understand the language, appears to be satirical. It keeps the sketches short and has energy. The team enjoy making the show and are intent on improving standards week by week. Morale is high and so are the ratings. *Gumaci* is the third most successful show in the Czech Republic. I was amused to notice they have even picked up on one of our trade secrets which is when short of material run a weatherman sketch (if writers cannot write a funny weatherman sketch it's time to find new writers).

I've not been to Japan to see the results of our franchise in Tokyo. Richard Bennett and one of the Spitting Image directors did go over to teach the Nippon team the tricks of the trade and brought back video tapes of how the show is made, including an interview with the Japanese programme makers and a short interview with Murray Sayle, a legendary Australian journalist who lives in Tokyo and writes about Japanese politics. Murray maintains the time is right for a Japanese *Spitting Image* as never before has so much sincerity been shown by Japanese politicians. He explained that "showing sincerity" was a euphemism for money changing hands. So no shortage of material in Japan. In the Japanese tapes I've seen there does not seem to be an awful lot of going for the jugular, but the production itself is a lesson to us all. Turning the sound off you really notice the team co-operation. It's most extraordinary – the puppeteers work in harmony, anticipating each other's moves. The tape of their very first show is more professional than anything we achieved in our first year. Maybe I should take out a franchise.

When Peter Fluck and I were working a millennium ago on the pilot of the British show, we were asked if we thought it would be successful. Peter thought it might be a cult success. I thought it would either die a death or be very successful. I did not think it was the kind of idea or show that people would be neutral about. It was not going to be the kind of TV that washes over you from the corner of the room like warmth from an electric fire. Neither of us thought it would catch on anywhere else, except perhaps in America. In the event, interest in the US has been more limited than in other parts of the world, though we have done shows for the main networks.

This year, we are hopefully taking TV franchises to the Brazilians, Argentinians, and South Africa. It seems the one bit of mischief that is genuinely universal is taking the piss out of politicians on TV.

Murayama
(Japan)

Designer printmaker

I came to Australia in 1961. At that time you couldn't get a line of type set properly, designers were paid £50 for a package design, the printer would do the job for free, and it was very much a case of "What do you need this guy for?" You were considered the oddball artist. There were only a few who had any sort of client/patron relationship, with one exception, Arthur Leydin, who realized that design was a business.

By the late 1960s, early 1970s, things started happening in Australia. It was around this time that Melbourne began making a name in world design. There were some wonderful people who wanted to show the world there were some good designers in Australia – Frank Eidlitz, Arthur Leydin, Lyn Waite, Garry Emery, Robert Rosetsky, John Nash, Brian Sadgrove and later, Barry Tucker. It was all fun, we drank and ate together and lived design. When Lyn Waite and I shared an office, we would have breakfast at six every morning bringing in books and discussing the whys and wheres – the philosophy of design.

But it seems to me today that the definition of graphic design is different than it was then.

Today everybody thinks they're a graphic designer, but it's more of a studio level. Good typography, photography, "me too" layout. I don't mind seeing the Dallas look, London look, Japanese look, but one should strive to do it better than they do it. Work that doesn't make it, needs more love. "Hard work love."

It takes long hours to produce a new look. I have spent thousands of hours moving type around, hoping to create a new space with type, with photos, with colour, lines, shapes.

Sometimes I would wonder if it was all worth it. Then I see someone's work who HAS made it all work!

In summary, I think there have been big changes in the world of design. Because of fast communications and excellent books all over the world, a much higher level of design has been created in countries big and small, and Australia has become part of this quality movement and a greater contributor.

In my work I am showing a thirty-year development, good or bad. I've tried to do a good job, sometimes more for myself than

Cover, *Epicurean*, magazine of Wine & Food Society, Australia, 1969

Print collage, Perth, West Australia, 1992

the client. But my belief was that I could do something to lift the level of design in the world. In my later years I am showing some of the work I always wanted to be involved in: printmaking, collage and spatial painting. I suppose that, over the years, space has become very important to me.

You could always create exciting work even if the message was not that important. I still love design but the client seems to have become less and somehow the level seems lower. Or maybe I am just becoming more philosophical.

SHIN MATSUNAGA

Japan

Harvest of boyhood dreams

Mainichi Shimbun, **8 March 1990**

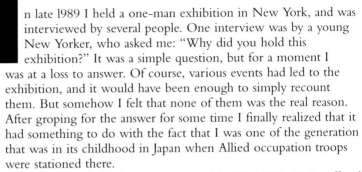

I n late 1989 I held a one-man exhibition in New York, and was interviewed by several people. One interview was by a young New Yorker, who asked me: "Why did you hold this exhibition?" It was a simple question, but for a moment I was at a loss to answer. Of course, various events had led to the exhibition, and it would have been enough to simply recount them. But somehow I felt that none of them was the real reason. After groping for the answer for some time I finally realized that it had something to do with the fact that I was one of the generation that was in its childhood in Japan when Allied occupation troops were stationed there.

For a period after Japan surrendered in World War II, it suffered serious shortages in food and all other goods. I was five when the war ended, and I saw occupation soldiers with an innocence as yet unsullied by school or urban society. I had nothing but admiration for the material superiority of the Americans, and that feeling is still implanted deep within me. Even after I became an adult and a professional, the urge to show my works to Americans – to show those "big brothers" just how much I had grown since those early postwar days – perhaps that was my greatest motive for giving the exhibition in the United States. Yet I only realized this after that simple question was asked. Apparently the young interviewer who asked the question understood this typically Japanese feeling of mine quite well. He listened quietly and happily, and I could see his eyes become wet, which impressed me all the more.

Soon after the war, we often saw American GIs and what was most memorable about them to me was the Lucky Strike cigarette packages they carried, their jeeps, the wrappings of chewing gum and Hershey chocolates they generously handed out to us children, as well as the colourful badges on their uniforms. A hungry little boy without a care for history or why the war was fought, I had hardly any idea of how bitterly the Japanese had fought the Americans and British for years, despising them as awful fiends. I was just dazzled by those badges and signs.

From the time I entered primary school I loved American films. Partly because there were few other diversions or entertainments

Lucky Strike, Raymond Loewy, 1940

Exhibition poster, "The works of
Shin Matsunaga New York 1989"

available to us children in the Chikuho area of Fukuoka prefecture
(Kyushu), where I spent most of my primary and junior high school
days, I saw many American movies. The films showed a shining,
dream-like world that might have been on a different planet. The
background for the title and credits of many of the films I saw
greatly impressed me, especially those for *The Man with the Golden
Arm*, *Around the World in 80 Days*, and *Bonjour Tristesse*. I later
learned that it was Saul Bass who designed many of those
backgrounds. So I grew up practically worshipping Bass, who is
active as a graphic designer in Los Angeles even today. Those were
among my first encounters with design. So, when Bass agreed to
contribute his comments to a published volume of my collected
works displayed in New York, I was deeply moved.

My experience is similar to that of many Japanese designers
of my generation. Totally without prejudice, we did not have
to be told in so many words what kind of design had punch and
power. We felt its raw power, as if through our very pores. This
is probably why the kind of designs I saw when I was young still
affect my work.

The impressions made on a young mind are like water soaking
into dry earth and they can determine the course of his or her
career. Those impressions and memories from the poverty-stricken
years in the wake of war are perhaps the greatest asset of my life.

ARMIN HOFMANN

Switzerland

Herbert Matter: a retrospective

Graphis, Nr. 212, Zürich, May/June 1981

The personality, work and career of Herbert Matter might well furnish stimulation and encouragement for a younger generation that is beginning to question the motives, aims and consequences of design more critically than was formerly the custom; but they would also supply plenty of food for thought.

Born in Engelberg, a Swiss mountain resort, Herbert Matter soon left the confined life of his native village to go to Geneva and study painting at the Ecole des Beaux-Arts. He continued these studies in Paris, where he was lucky enough to meet Fernand Léger and Amédée Ozenfant. His confrontation with Léger's work, philosophy and working methods was no doubt a major event in Matter's life and helped to decide his artistic evolution. Even though he moved gradually away from painting to photography and graphic design, the criteria that he had learnt to apply to painting were to retain their validity throughout his later life.

To understand Herbert Matter's espousal of applied art, we must remember that in the 1930s graphic design seemed to offer a widening of creative scope rather than any limitation. His meeting with A M Cassandre and Le Corbusier may also have led him to see the mastering of problems affecting daily life as the more urgent task. In New York, which soon became his second home, he found the wide field of activity that best suited his temperament and that still keeps him on his toes.

As in Paris, he soon established contact with a circle of friends that included the painters of the New York scene in 1960: Jackson Pollock, Willem de Kooning, Franz Kline, Philip Guston, Alexander Calder and others. Among them he found confirmation of his own intentions and aims, he discussed his work on new projects with them and began to be aware of the great importance of the teaching he had already embarked upon.

Herbert Matter is in many ways – as a graphic designer, a photographer, a film-maker, a teacher, a critic – an exception to the rule. If the aspect of his work that first surprises the observer is his insistence on clean design, on clarity of utterance, on the original use of lettering and image, it must be added that he also harbours a deep mistrust of everything specious and superficial.

Sequences to an educational film with letter i. Armin Hofmann, *Graphic Design Manual*, Arthur Niggli Ltd., 1965, CH-9052 Niederteufen, Switzerland

He endeavoured from the very first to close the gap that threatened to open between the higher aims of art and the lower standards that to many seemed adequate for the everyday uses of applied design. He was uniquely successful in giving the artistic development of photography a place in his graphic activities and in ensuring its validity in practical life. He sought, with a perseverance equalled by very few of his colleagues, the narrow and difficult path between the shaping area we tend to think of as fine art and that we have come to connect with requirements of modern advertising.

Design formulations of such experimental verve as we find in the posters for the Swiss National Tourist Office, in the Knoll advertisements and in the brochures done for a printing house would have been unthinkable if the aim had been merely the maximum economic effect. In the course of his years in New York, a conception based on a humanist philosophy of how modern man should react to word and image took an ever more distinct form in his mind. It was on the strength of this vision that he made the very finely conceived Calder film, that he began the preparatory work for the educational film about Buckminster Fuller, compiled the magnificent book on Alberto Giacometti and perfected his photographic work.

Although Herbert Matter left his home country unconditionally in his early youth, it would be quite wrong to interpret this as a flight. On the contrary, it seems as though – just like Giacometti – he was better able, in the far-off city, to grasp and process the deep impressions the mountain world had left upon his spirit. In his character, his outward appearance and his behaviour, Herbert Matter remained a son of the mountains – quiet, modest, thorough and very critical. These are no doubt qualities that made him such a success as a professor at Yale University. For apart from his high qualifications as a photographer, he was able to reply to the ever-repeated questions of his students as to which was the right path to take with the example set by his own life. As a teacher he has always been revered and loved; as an artist and photographer he ranks among pioneers.

WOLFGANG WEINGART

Switzerland

Mendell & Oberer: no gags

Unpublished, Basle, 1988

Mendell & Oberer are vestiges of a particular era when both craftsmanship and visual aesthetics were still respected parts of the design profession at its highest level. The anachronism may be partially a result of their exceptional training; they met each other and were both visually awakened in a Swiss design institution which still maintains an outstanding international reputation for its educational programme: the Basle School of Design. At the age of eighteen, Klaus Oberer began a graphic apprenticeship at school. Pierre Mendell, who was a bit older, came to Switzerland from the United States. During the late 1950s they worked with the same teachers and completed the same programme. There, they were able to grow and experiment in a creative laboratory of ideas under the direction of such didactic personalities as Emil Ruder and Armin Hofmann.

Certainly there were many reasons to open a studio in a city other than Basle, somewhere which had then and has now nothing to do with Switzerland. Munich is a baroque and complex metropolis with as much flourish as tradition. Everyday life is typified by Schweinshaxe and beer, and visitors pile out of tour buses to throng to the Hofbräuhaus and to be photographed in front of the city hall. The yearly calendar of events crescendos with the city's carnival and Oktoberfest. These were not the reasons, however, to select this location to risk opening a new studio. Mendell & Oberer knew instead that there is much more to Munich: it is also a city of theatres, splendid museums, comfortable little galleries, and the internationally known English Gardens. This is not the least of it: there are also factories, the industries, the art dealers, the elegant department stores, and the city residents with their high standards of culture who maintain Munich's centuries of tradition in music and the arts. Is it not more than coincidence that even Mozart lived not far away, in Salzburg? Ultimately, the real reason to move to Munich was that Michael Engelmann, the intelligent graphic revolutionary of Germany during the 1950s and 1960s, was there. Were it not for him, Mendell & Oberer might now be in New York, Los Angeles or Sydney.

My first visit to their Munich studio was in 1963, when I was

43

twenty-three years old. I remember it well; their work was totally unintelligible to me. At that time, I still had all the simplicity and limitations of a farmer-village mentality. My visual world was conditioned by the hallowed precepts of centre-axis typography and decadent art philosophies, and the confusion of post-war poster design cluttered my mental landscape. German art professors of the era had continued to teach calligraphy, woodcut and linocut just in the same way that these subjects had been instructed since the 1930s, and students like myself dutifully made symbols and designed posters with brushes and quill pens under the watchful eyes of teachers such as Brudi, Schneidler and Trump.

When I was asked to write an introduction to this catalogue, I thought it would be very easy to jot down a little story about their beautiful work. I have never had so much difficulty writing about a theme. Why the problem? One of many answers could be that I am jealous of the intelligence and serene wisdom of their results. And why write long stories about something that is so beautiful in its simplicity anyway? In this chaotic western world, I cannot find one other person who duplicates the language of this studio. Every piece of theirs is a masterpiece, every work is a Stradivarius. When I open a 1984/1985 *form* magazine and see the double-page advertisements for Schlagheck & Schultes Design, I breathe in a generosity, an intelligence, and just an eloquent minimum of typography and colour. This freshness and directness are the product of minds cleaned out by a strong thunderstorm, in which every last possible corner of graphic tastelessness and kitsch has been washed away by an unforgiving rain. No gags, no fads, no mimicry of current fashion; no ornament which makes no sense. This purity rises above the smog of the ordinary to its own level of timelessness. We see, in the final analysis, that success does not depend upon complexity.

The person who looks at this work and simply dismisses it as being too cold in attitude, too intellectual, or not understandable, is someone who cannot see any more. This person's capacity to understand the importance of abstraction has been spoiled by the world of almost-pictures, the easy illusions of television and video and magazines. This human being is tragically deafened to the intelligence of simplicity and the eloquence of minimality. And the sound of a Stradivarius is pure yet weighty indeed.

HENRY STEINER

Hong Kong

Thoughts on Paul Rand

1988

A girl design student was reduced to tears, several other classmates were flabbergasted at being treated in a cold analytical manner, there were hurt sensibilities and anger, but I was enthralled: Paul Rand was giving his first critique of a graphic design class assignment in the Yale Art and Architecture School. It was the autumn of 1956.

Josef Albers, the former Bauhaus instructor, was running the Art School. Optical discoveries seemed to glimmer in every painter's cubicle. Abstract geometric color studies were the norm, figurative art was virtually *verboten*.

In the basement of Louis Kahn's elegantly spare concrete building, the class of '57 studied printmaking with Gabor Peterdi, photography with Herbert Matter, editorial layout with Bradbury Thompson. The graphic design department was headed by Alvin Eisenman whose tall, gangling presence was everywhere at once. He had started the department five years earlier and still heads it as I write this. He had a lanky body and a habit of staring at the ceiling, perhaps seeking inspiration. His nickname among the students was Ichabod Crane, after the character in Washington Irving's *Legend of Sleepy Hollow*. He had the astonishing ability of identifying unfailingly the place of manufacture anywhere in the world of any blank scrap of paper a student presented to him.

After college in 1955 I had enrolled in the Graphic Design MFA program at Yale. At the end of my first year Alvin announced that Paul Rand would be joining the staff in the Fall term. I was overjoyed at the news.

Rand's posters had brightened the dull section of Manhattan where I grew up. In my high school and college years I was aware of the Interfaith Day posters in the subway, the El Producto cigar boxes displayed in the candy stores, the advertisements for Ohrbach's in *The New York Times*. In the Public Library on East 23rd Street I discovered Paul's classic book *Thoughts on Design* with the splendid abacus photogram on the cover. I marvelled at the erudition of the text and was charmed by the witty visuals.

At Yale Paul always wore a jacket and tie to his weekly classes. The tie was invariably a black knitted one: once he wore it with a

45

Maquette, Henry Steiner
portfolio piece, Yale, 1958

bright red shirt, an unusually bold sartorial statement for those decorous Eisenhower years. He was short and had a boxer's head, massive, pugnacious, with close-cropped hair and a bristling energy about him. He wore glasses and his eyes twitched frequently; we nicknamed him Blinky. He was forty-two years old.

He spoke with a Brooklyn accent from his boyhood but with many scholarly allusions and frequent *mots justes*. His command of art history and philosophy were formidable and in any given session he might cite Corbusier, Henry James, Ozenfant, Tschichold, or AN Whitehead to make a point.

Once he digressed to demonstrate how enclosing a figure within a shape could energize it and drew upon Aristide Maillol's signature as an example. This inspired me to create my own monogram. On another occasion he explained how the more sparingly one used a second color, "the more precious – in the good sense – it becomes".

His method was to assign the redesign of an existing advertisement, poster or trademark. Along with our design, we had to write an explanation of the idea behind it on a 3" by 5" index card. The first assignment was to redesign an advertisement for cooking chocolate. The following week the index card requirement proved to be a stumbling block to many of my classmates who were unable to set down an idea. They talked of "shapes" and the girl who wept had described a "feeling" of Alice in Wonderland. She totally lost her composure when Rand said "If you don't have an idea, you don't have a design".

Along with the concept of requiring an idea at the start of the design process, Rand gave me another valued intellectual tool. This was contrast, which he said was the heart of any good design. It could be contrast of big and small, old and new, strange and familiar. He arrived at this theory based on his knowledge of Hegelian dialectics, Chinese Yin/Yang, Japanese Zen, and a smattering of Ecclesiastes.

As the school year continued we received other assignments: a corporate identity for US Lines, a poster for Italy, an announcement for a painter's exhibition.

In his critiques, with one observation, Rand was able to make a design more effective. He did this in one case by blanking out an area with his hand, in another by turning a poster upside down. During one particular session, Rand relentlessly criticized and corrected the displayed posters in his intellectually honest and dispassionate manner. As he went through our creations, I kept waiting for his assessment of one which looked especially outstanding, but others seemed to occupy his attention. Finally a classmate, in a spirit of fairness, asked him why he had not commented on the poster which I admired. Paul seemed taken aback and replied: "I have nothing to say about it. It's a fine design." I believe his valid concern at that time was with improving weaker designs rather than complimenting achievement.

He once observed that any colors could be made to work together if they were separated by white or black bands, referring to Matisse and the windows of Chartres. The assistant lecturer for Paul's course was Norman Ives, a disciple of Albers and his painstaking approach to the interaction of color. Norman sniffed: "Well, that's taking the easy way out." Rand shot back: "If you can do it the easy way, why do it the hard way?" A confrontation between Yankee idealism and Brooklyn pragmatism. (Rand respected Albers, however, and affectionately quoted his German accented definition of an intentionally designed optical trick as a "schvindle".)

Most of my classmates were happier puttering with arrangements of the 19th-century wooden type fonts Alvin had collected for the school. They were initially unhappy with his cerebral, Apollonian approach to the assessment of their work, but I perceived that Rand was attempting to instil in us a rigor of analysis, a rational method of creation that he had achieved by studying the process in himself. Certainly, several of us were spurred on to producing the best work we could.

I made an effort to get to know Paul better. This resulted in an invitation to visit his home in Weston, a short train ride south from New Haven.

He was behind the house, clearing some fallen branches and pulling out weeds near the edge of his property. I helped him with this humble rustic activity. It was early autumn and still warm.

After a while we went into the kitchen where he drank a mixture of seltzer and orange juice; a fizzy combination which he recommended as being very thirst-quenching. He said he needed to be active and speculated that if he were in jail without the possibility of doing something constructive, of effecting change, he would probably kill himself.

Several years before, Rand had bought this lovely, undulating piece of land and built a charming house in the spare International Style with a flavor of Charles Eames and Japanese architecture.

It was a one-storey structure and consisted of large square white walls and clear glass panels which enclosed some spaces and allowed vistas from others. Inside it one had a sense of being pleasantly removed from the rest of the world. It was furnished with classic contemporary furniture, a zebra skin on a tile floor and several small paintings by modern masters. I recall a Picasso, a Klee, and there may have been a Miró – all artists who exerted an influence on Rand. The exception to this unarguable pantheon was a painting by Richard Lindner, a friend of Paul's. There was also a painting by Paul of an overburdened burro, on which he later based an illustration for one of his children's books. There was a

Magazine cover,
Henry Steiner, Paris, 1959

47

studio wing to the building. A lithograph by Le Corbusier was on the wall. Paul worked here and had one assistant who came on weekdays. At the time he was drawing in his happy linear style an anthropomorphic cigar dressed as a big game hunter who had just bagged a lion.

Paul had been a *wunderkind*, becoming art editor of *Esquire* magazine in New York at the age of eighteen and setting a standard which would be maintained later by Henry Wolf. He then worked for Wm H Weintraub and Co. with Bill Bernbach who would subsequently start Doyle Dane Bernbach, an agency which set new standards for creativity in the 1950s and 1960s.

When I met Paul he had been working freelance for several years. His most recent coup was the IBM corporate identity. He was receiving a retainer of $10,000 a year as graphic consultant to the company which was then graduating from electric typewriters to computers.

At his home, Rand spoke with wonder about Saul Bass having called him long distance all the way from California to invite him to judge an exhibition on the West Coast. He was flattered because Bass was a design superstar at the time. In New Haven we would see his pioneering film titles for *A Walk on the Wild Side, Anatomy of a Murder, The Man with the Golden Arm*, etc.

I had been to New York with my class a few weeks before to view the 1956 AIGA show, which seemed to break new ground in graphic design. I was enthusiastic about the work of Herb Lubalin, but Rand found his stacked capitals a bit "zippy".

At another time he was rather scathing about the typography of what he called the "Swiss yodelers". Later, due to a friendship with Josef Müller-Brockmann he underwent a Pauline conversion (comparable to Stravinsky's embracing of the tone row method of composition). Thereafter, his work and teaching included a lively interest in the grid system of layout. This was seen in his IBM annual reports of the early 1960s with their meticulous *raster* layouts and sensitive Garamond typography. The latter marked another change in Paul's work, as before then he tended to rely heavily on either Futura or Bodoni.

Magazine advertisement,
Agence SNIP, Henry Steiner
Paris, 1960

Paul once described to me how, when he was working on the IBM identity, he kept going through type specimen books, until he hit on the German 1930s "City" typeface. He modified it to produce the famous logo; eventually he produced the present, striped version.

During one of his critiques he mentioned how important it was to move elements around on a page until one found the right positioning and how this could take hours or days. Behind the seemingly nonchalant spontaneity of Paul's work lies much scholarship, thought and patient effort.

A friend once remarked on Paul's apparent self-absorption,

New Year greeting card,
Henry Steiner, Hong Kong, 1962

saying that at dinner the conversation with Rand went dead unless it centred on what Paul was doing or thought. There may be some truth to this observation, but then if one were privileged to have a conversation with, say, Gutenberg, would it not be silly to waste time discussing the price of cabbages in Mainz?

Once during that school year he brought to a class Raymond Savignac, the great Parisian *affichiste*, introducing him with relish for a language in which he was not at home, as "*mon cher confrère*". He also achieved a passable British accent in describing a visit to Henri Henrion's London club a previous summer. Henrion claims that when he introduced Rand to Eisenman at the club, the subject of a visiting professorship was broached and Paul's first question was "How much?"

I have mentioned the influence on Paul's house of Japanese architecture. He also treasured a plain cylindrical jardinière covered in a regular pattern of neat blue Chinese calligraphy. Soon after arriving in Hong Kong I bought an identical piece of porcelain, one of the few objects I would never abandon if I were to leave Asia.

Rand's interest in Asia was more theoretical than empirical: he made only one short visit to Japan. I was told of his mischievous wit at a geisha party during that trip when one of the girls asked him where he came from. Realizing the difficulty the Japanese have with certain consonants, he gave not his real place of origin but Brattleboro, a town in Vermont. The three syllables of this word form a perfect shibboleth for the Japanese and all the geisha were tongue-tied attempting its pronunciation.

Paul had to relinquish the professorial position at Yale when he passed the age of seventy, but he continues to teach the "master classes" which Alvin created and at the Yale summer school in Brissago in Italian Switzerland.

I know that Paul never intended to cause distress to his classes but he felt it his duty to challenge and to improve. Many design students expect a teacher to disinterestedly "bless" their offerings. This indulgent attitude has led to the distressingly low standard of professional ability shown by the majority of design graduates today. As a teacher, Paul was simply thoroughly involved with and absorbed in his profession. Others dabble at their work, Paul lives as a consummate designer, creating his environment, meeting admired colleagues, reading widely but with relevance to his calling.

He remains wholly dedicated to his craft and continues to live totally as the archetypal graphic designer of our time. In Milton Glaser's words, "He keeps us honest."

I understand he has modified his technique so that rather than discuss the displayed homework with all the class present, he now has private tutorials with one designer at a time in his office. Kinder and more face-saving perhaps, but what a loss of opportunity to learn from each other's successes and failures,

to watch a master swiftly rearrange a composition to improve its
message, to observe him doggedly challenge a design student on
his line of reasoning and find an idea hidden in the piece.

Paul's gruelling critiques proved invaluable for his students
and during his thirty years Yale produced a remarkable number
of outstanding designers. Once you had learned from Paul to
analyse the problem, to articulate your solution and to be prepared
to defend it in the face of his relentless probing, you were ready
to face any client presentation with serene confidence.

On two recent stays in New York I was privileged to breakfast
with Paul and his wife Marion (who had been manager of design
for IBM) at the Yale Club during their overnight visits to
Manhattan. Marion has slightly softened Paul's pugnacity though
his tight helmet of hair is white but still bristling. His work remains
vigorous; his latest, most notable project is the identity for Steven
Jobs' company, Next. At the most recent breakfast our conversation
turned to Paul's religion. He is not only a born Jew, but a devout
one. While I now hardly enter a synagogue, even for the high holy
days, Marion remarked that Paul not only attends *Schul* but prays
at home daily in the ancient, prescribed manner.

"Well," he explained, "it keeps me humble."

My reply was: "Paul, perhaps you need it more than I do."

SHIGEO FUKUDA

Japan

Raymond Savignac

Creation, no. 2, Japan, 1989

R aymond Savignac is more than simply one of France's leading graphic designers. More accurately he might be described as one of the most important contemporary artists to figure prominently in the history of poster art. Savignac's posters span across no less than half a century. His uncommon talent has brought untold pleasure to poster enthusiasts not only throughout Europe but throughout the entire world. At the same time he has also provided a constant and powerful stimulus that piques the sensibilities of the world's graphic designers and gives them the courage to imagine and create.

Savignac's works have customarily been accorded such descriptive labels as "visual shock", "visual scandal", "explosive humour", or "shocked laughter". All these terms contain an element of negativism which disqualifies them as epithets of unbridled praise, and this negative trace probably reflects the bewilderment experienced by most viewers. Seen in a different light, Savignac's works perhaps succeed in shocking us so powerfully because they trespass beyond the limits of our common sense.

Consider his depiction of a pig being sliced into ham and the "shocked laughter" which it elicits from us. Unwittingly, the look of joy in the pig's eyes somehow overlaps with the expression in the face of the man depicted in a work Savignac exhibited in this year's international poster show, held in commemoration of the 200th anniversary of the French Revolution. In the latter the man, wearing trousers in the colours of the French flag, is taking wing over ominously dark clouds. It boggles the mind to think that Savignac's pig poster was first exhibited as long as forty years ago.

The "unchanging" nature of Savignac's approach to creativity is of great importance. In fact, in the context of contemporary graphic design, to find the same images in one artist's works spanning forty years is nothing short of miraculous – and it is in this respect that Savignac's talent is truly unique.

Savignac recently came into the spotlight in Japan when a local advertisement featuring one of his illustrations won a prize in an advertising contest. What is especially interesting to note is that this

recent flourish of acclaim was in no way linked to Savignac's stature as an 82-year-old grand master of worldwide renown, but rather derived from what was viewed as his dashing vitality as a "rookie" illustrator. This too is an indication of his uncommon "talent". Also, attention was showered on Savignac because of his individual talent, instead of putting spotlighting on some new approach or transformation – a rare occurrence in a world that typically reveres advanced information technology far above the often neglected realm of humour.

Throughout Savignac's life he has continuously sought the answer to the question of "what a designer should do". Through humour he has long pioneered the difficult path toward the summit of his craft, a peak in the art of visual communication which he is now on the verge of reaching. The ultimate object of his quest, however, is not just to elicit a wry smile through humour or "visual scandal". Rather, he seeks to create a new form of "culture" that will add depth and interest to our human lives.

HELMUT SCHMID

Germany/Japan

Emil Ruder: Rikyu of typography

Typographische Monatsblaetter, no. 3, Switzerland, 1971

**"You place the charcoal so that the water boils properly and
you make the tea to bring out the proper taste.
You arrange the flowers as they appear when they are growing.
In summer you suggest coolness and in winter cosiness."**

Senno Rikyu's preference for the natural produced a lasting impression on the arts. Rikyu, tea-master of the sixteenth century, is a legendary figure today if only because he himself left nothing in writing. Emil Ruder left us his essential contributions to questions on typography, *Wesentliches* in four parts and a design manual entitled *Typographie.* His dynamic personality, however, really only became apparent during his lectures.

Surprisingly enough it was quite easy to join Ruder's private course on typography. He was not interested in notes or in specimens. Sketches were not necessary. The copy was set and proofed, then the cut lines of type formed a composition in a given space.

"The oriental philosophers hold that the essence of created form depends on empty space. Without its hollow interior a jug is merely a lump of clay, and it is only the empty space inside that makes it into a vessel." Ruder's interpretation of the eleventh aphorism from the *Tao Te Ching* is an interpretation of his own typography. He demonstrated for years that only the surrounding space puts life into the printed.

"The 'i' is usually the best letter in a typeface" is Ruder's answer to the numerous typefaces offered by the type foundaries. With Univers he saw his ideas come true. His contribution to the creation of Univers made him not only the prophet of this typeface but also of its typography. Ruder's philosophy and appearance is comparable to that of the greatest of all tea-masters. Rikyu arranged the stepping stones of the *roji* – the path to the tea-house – in such a way that they appeared to be first of all functional, but at the same time they were equally aesthetic. The path of Miyokian, a private tea-house outside Kyoto, thought to be arranged by Rikyu, is so simple that one does not think of it as being designed. Like Rikyu, Ruder aspired to the natural, the simple, the useful.

"The flowers depart while we hate to lose them, the weeds arrive while we hate to watch them grow."

53

PAULA SCHER

USA

The boat

Print, **New York, May 1993**

Recently, the following letters were exchanged between Julie Lasky, managing editor of PRINT, and Paula Scher, partner in the New York office of Pentagram Design and former art director of CBS Records. Lasky's letter has been edited for brevity: Scher's is reproduced in its entirety:

Dear Paula,

Thumbing through the latest AIGA annual, we ran across the picture of Pentagram's partners gathered together on a boat on the Thames and couldn't help noticing that you were the only woman in the group. Then we recalled that the art department at CBS Records wasn't a bastion of feminism, either.

How would you feel about writing 1000 or so words for us on the subject of breaking into and working for the boys' clubs? (I know it's not an original topic, but you always provide an original point of view.) Has your experience in the male dominated Pentagram of the early 1990s been different from working in the male-dominated CBS Records in the early 1980s and before? Have you ever suffered tokenism? At the Chicago AIGA Conference last year, Cheryl Heller remarked that being the lone woman among male professionals brought an element of surprise that worked to her advantage: she could easily soar above the low expectations of her colleagues and clients. Has this been your experience? Does your status as a woman executive bring more responsibility in terms of mentoring other women both within and beyond your workplace? Do you consider yourself a role model? Has role-modelling been thrust upon you? Please let me know.

Sincerely,
Julie Lasky
Managing Editor, *Print*

Dear Julie,

I've long resisted the notion of writing a "woman's issue" piece, or what it's like to be the only woman blah-blah. I'm genuinely uncomfortable with the subject because I have conflicting feelings about it. I'd have to have been an ostrich not to have experienced the painful exclusivity of corporate boys' clubs, glass ceilings, and financial exploitation. I can sing along with any woman's group about the sexist-insensitive-noncommunicative-emotionally-inept nature of men and add a few two-syllable adjectives of my own for good measure. But my confusion comes not in the worthy politicizing of women's issues, but in their valid application to a life spent working in graphic design.

Every time I give a presentation to a design group, I'm asked what it's like to be a woman blah-blah. As I'm invited to give the presentation, I'm told that women will really want to hear about being a woman blah-blah. I estimate that 60 per cent of the calls I receive to speak or judge are related to woman blah-blah. They go like this: "Hello, can you judge the annual Peoria Hang-Tag competition, please say yes because we need a female juror." How I envy my male partners who are invited to speak based on their achievements and prestige as opposed to their sex. I cannot separate my own achievements from being a woman blah-blah.

On the other hand, the tokenism has had its advantages. I've been able to attain a visibility that might have been harder to come by if I were male. The visibility may be helpful professionally, but it's always clouded in a veil of "women's issues". How ironic that the grand attempt in the graphic community to promote women designers serves to undermine and diminish achievement.

The thing of it is, I never set out to be the only woman blah-blah. I set out to be a designer. I set out to be a designer who could design all kinds of things well, with the hope that those things that I designed well would lead me to even more things to design. I set out as a designer, not thinking that being a woman had much to do with anything. What mattered was the work. After all, designers produce tangible products. You can *see* the results. There is physical evidence of success or failure. I believed that good work brought more good work and that money, while dictated by marketplace, could mushroom, to a degree, in relationship to good work and reputation. I've held these beliefs for twenty years. I've had to, or I would not have been able to continue to work. The ability to continually produce work, make professional changes, take advantage of opportunities as they arise, and create opportunities yourself when they don't arise is key to the growth and development of a designer, male or female.

I don't believe that pursuing this course while happening to be a woman is particularly special, nor do I believe there should be a special standard for women. I haven't "broken" into boys' clubs. I am merely following the path of a life in design at a time when doors are opening for women, not merely because they are women, but because they are successfully following that path.

Which brings me to the photograph of the Pentagram partners on the boat. It is interesting how one photographic image can perfectly encapsulate my feelings. You said you couldn't help noticing that I was the only woman on the boat. I was less interested in the fact that I was the only woman; I already knew that. I was struck more by the pure visual physicality of the situation - not the oddity of the sex, but the strangeness in scale. There I am, halfway down the side of the boat in between rugged

The Pentagram partners on the Thames, England, 22 May 1992: from bow to stern, Michael Bierut, Kenneth Grange, Alan Fletcher, John Rushworth, Peter Harrison, Theo Crosby, Mervyn Kurlansky, Peter Saville, David Hillman, Paula Scher, Kit Hinrichs, James Biber, Woody Pirtle, Neil Shekery, Colin Forbes, John McConnell, Lowell Williams. Photo by Peter Harrison

David Hillman and James Biber, who is twice my size. Kit Hinrichs, who is actually sitting behind James Biber, has a head that is half as large as mine. And Colin Forbes, who stands with John McConnell and Lowell Williams, way in the back, appears much larger than me. I look like a person who was originally standing far beyond Lowell Williams, and was then stripped into the middle of the photograph but not blown up in proportion to the new position.

The photograph has made me look at my own professional situation, and those of other women today, as a matter of strange scale. I'm in the picture, but I'm not blown up in proportion to the new position. (If the photograph had pictured the same number of men and women, the scale wouldn't be strange, I'd just be short.)

I saw a similar thing in the *New York Times* several weeks ago. There was Donna Shalala standing next to Bill Clinton and Al Gore and some male senators and newly appointed Cabinet members and she was not blown up in proportion to her new position. The same week in the same *New York Times*, I read about how women's groups were upset with Clinton for not appointing enough women to Cabinet posts and Clinton railed against the quotas. All of this served to diminish the wonderful accomplishments of the excellent women who were appointed. One woman in the group. Two women in the group. Their individuality is lost and all one sees is the strangeness of scale.

I'm physically odd at Pentagram, the way I'm physically odd at a corporate meeting with clients who happen to be men. I'm physically odd to women who work for men in groups and view me as out of scale to the men in those groups.

I joined Pentagram the way I set out to design. I had a business with one male partner for seven years. We had been split for one year and I had continued running the business myself. I was offered the opportunity to join Pentagram and I took it because I wanted to design things well and get more new things to design. There's no more to it than that. No crusade, no breaking down back room doors. I took some personal risk, with the price being the daily discomfort of being out of scale.

I can't equate Pentagram and CBS Records. Pentagram is a group of very intelligent, talented and relatively sensitive men who design well and want to get more new things to design. I may be out of scale at Pentagram, but I was out of sync at CBS Records. That's much worse than being out of scale. One doesn't have to be a woman to be out of sync. All that requires is for one to have a completely different set of values than the larger group. Being out of scale can be uncomfortable. Being out of sync is dangerous. Women need to learn the difference.

It seems to me from your letter, particularly in reference to

Cheryl Heller's talk, that you are looking for some sort of *modus operandi* for surviving in male-dominated working situations. There isn't one. Men are different. Situations are different. And women are different. The only thing that is constant for me is my relationship to my work. When I find myself in a professional situation that is purely about politics or personalities and not about the effectiveness of design, I tend to fail.

Which brings me back to my ambiguous feelings about women's issues in relationship to design. A profession that has been long dominated by men is changing. There are simply more women. There are more women who are terrific designers, more women running their own businesses, more women changing the scale of things and appearing out of scale in the process.

There are also more underpaid women, more women juggling careers and motherhood, more women who feel squeezed out in a bad economy, more women going to art school and going nowhere afterwards, and more women who are resentful of their lack of success "because they are women".

There are more women in design groups, more women's panels, more women mentoring women, more women who want women to mentor them, more women looking for women role models, and more women who don't like other women's success.

I don't know what my responsibility is in all this. I'm not sure I have one as it relates to women in general. There are things I've done naturally through relationships that existed by chance. I felt supportive of the terrific women designers at CBS Records because they were my friends. I have encouraged talented students, male and female, equally. I've supported those people I know and cared about who want to design well and get more things to design. It is not a planned activity, or a duty; it is simply part of a life in design.

I don't want to be anyone's "role model". I dislike the term because it diminishes my life by implying that I'm playing some kind of role for other people's benefit. It places my entire life out of scale. This takes me back to the picture on the boat, where I'm confronted with my own image within a group. The boat ride on the Thames was really lovely. There was a good lunch, terrific conversation, and all in all the most pleasant part of an exhausting partners meeting. I don't remember feeling like an oddity on that boat. But in the photo there is that strangeness of scale.

Women's issues in design are focused on scale. We count the numbers, look at the statistics, and demand change, and all the while change is occurring. Change doesn't come in one great thump. It comes one by one by one by one, and it looks kind of funny. And then it doesn't.

Sincerely,
Paula Scher
Partner, Pentagram Design, Inc.

Henryk Tomaszewski

Creation, no. 6, Japan, 1990

Henryk TOMASZEWSKI Varsovie
Société des Beaux-Arts · Palais des Congrès
Kunstverein Kongresshaus Biel-Bienne (Foyer)
21 juin - 30 juillet 1969 · 21.Juni - 30.Juli 1969

Exhibition poster, 1968

Theatre poster, 1986

The very first time I saw the work of Henryk Tomaszewski in person, at a one-man showing in Warsaw, I was awakened by an abrupt shock. It was the same tingling sort of sensation that a Zen novitiate experiences when his master raps him across the shoulder with a slat of bamboo to keep him from letting worldly thoughts disturb meditation on deeper truths.

Tomaszewski's brushstrokes struck me like lightning. They bolted off their canvas and stunned me with their piercing playfulness. They captivated me with their explicit charm.

Seeing Tomaszewski's works assembled before me like this for the first time, I suddenly realized that there is even more meaning in them than I had previously perceived. In their every brushstroke they contain the same spiritual concentration demanded of the finest calligrapher. In their concise messages they harbour the poetic profundity of a seventeen-syllable haiku. In their microcosmic simplicity they convey the same infinite world as a single flower arranged in solitude.

The exhibition hall was filled with an almost palpable cosmos transcending individual sensibilities. Together with the crowds that thronged to see Tomaszewski's works that day, it floated through the corridors of the gallery.

Tomaszewski was standing authoritatively, with dignity, in the centre of the hall. He was surrounded by a collection of people who had gathered to experience the grand euphonic harmony of his works and to meet the man of fertile imagination and vibrant energy who had created them.

Spying me out of the corner of his eye, Tomaszewski held up his hand and bade me welcome. Perhaps my initial perception had been correct, for indeed he seemed to have the air of a Zen monk. His face glowed with a healthy colour, outward proof of his inner peace and satisfaction with his vocational endeavours.

Tomaszewski is a native of Poland, a nation that experienced unimaginable torment during World War II. Yet throughout those tumultuous years he managed to forge his own style well ahead of its time, a style which subsequently exerted a powerful influence on the normally fickle world of graphic design.

As is well known, Poland has long been an ideal breeding ground for poster design. It is in Poland that many young designers have had their start and inspiration, moving on from there to establish themselves among Europe's top graphic designers, where they continue to comprise a formidable mainstream even today.

What sets Tomaszewski apart from his contemporaries, in addition to his remarkable foresight and passionate contributions as an educator, is that he inhabits one of the peaks of graphic design history. It is a peak on which he meditates, Zen-style, on the vagaries on this earthly world.

Tomaszewski approached me carrying a great bouquet of roses from one of his admirers. As he greeted me, he graciously placed one of them in my lapel... like arranging a single flower.

BENNO WISSING

USA

Paul Schuitema

Typographica **8, London, December 1963**

Paul Schuitema – typographical designer, photographer, film maker, architect and teacher – was born at Groningen in northern Holland in 1897. He received his formal training as a painter during the period of the First World War. But it was the exciting developments of the immediate post-war years which determined the course of his future activities.

The ripples emanating from the Russian revolution overturned many old values and conceptions. Artists and scientists discovered new opportunities. The events of that period moved rapidly, and this, perhaps, explains the extraordinary consistency of many of the exploits of those days. The notion of *l'art pour l'art* by which earlier generations of artists had dissociated themselves from the social structure had no appeal for the young painters, writers and architects of 1918. It was not futurism or cubism that brought the artist back to reality, but the ideas released by the October Revolution.

In Moscow, in *The Realistic Manifesto* of August 1920, Gabo and Pevsner declared "life does not know beauty as an aesthetic measure... efficacious existence is the highest beauty. Life knows neither good nor bad nor justice as a measure of morals... need is the highest and most just of all morals. Life does not know rationally abstracted truths as a measure of cognizance, deed is the highest and surest of truths."

Architects, writers, composers and painters, aware that they had a definite function to perform and spurning spurious self-expressionism, broke away from the aesthetic laws of the Renaissance and denounced formalism. They discovered dynamic new media and sought to realize their ends by technological means. They rejected as romanticism the handicraft standards of the past.

Men like Heartfield, Piet Zwart, Moholy-Nagy, Lissitzky and Schuitema devised both the message and the technique used to convey that message. As artists, they knew that in order to convey their messages clearly and concisely they must evolve an effective technique. The writings of Mondrian, Moholy-Nagy, Gabo and Schuitema at this time are extraordinarily direct. They did not beat about the bush. The style is raw, sometimes angry, but the message is unmistakably clear. They adapted techniques to suit their immediate purpose. When they employed photographs, they did so not for photography's sake, but to make the message real, concrete and international. They utilized old typefaces but released them from their horizontal strait-jacket. They invented methods to project several dimensions. Depth and space entered their language. They found ways of relaying simultaneousness, action and counteraction. The edges of the page were no longer the limits of the printed message.

In an article in *Neue Grafik* (No. 11) Schuitema wrote: "It was essential that our designs should be taut and arresting. The first and most important colour to us was red. Blue and yellow came later. We always used primary colours, never mixtures. We favoured sanserif type: condensed and spaced, bold and light. These were the principles on which we worked. Photomontage was equally important to us. We applied the photograph freely to the flat rectangular surface, never making use of proportion or of drawing for that would have been too much like painting. If we drew we abstracted or simplified as much as possible and went straight for the objective without any romantic trimmings."

Schuitema sought to weld photographic elements into his designs for printed matter but, working with professional photographers, he found his efforts frustrated by their formalism and artistic individualism. He therefore taught himself, by trial and error, the processes of photography and he soon began to cherish the effects of motion he was able to capture in a photograph. Visitors to the 1927 *Bild und Foto* exhibition in Stuttgart were deeply impressed by Schuitema's photograms and montages. Photography forms a potent part of Schuitema's printed designs of the years between 1926 and 1933.

Much of his work of this period was for Berkel, to whom he acted as adviser, and besides designing many booklets and folders, he devised the Berkel trademark, laid out their stationery, and planned their showrooms and exhibition stands. And he influenced the design of their products, too – and simplified production – by severely reducing the number of basic components in their cutting and weighing machines.

About this time he also established, with the collaboration of two friends, a factory for the production of tubular steel furniture of his design. This enterprise prospered but Schuitema found that it absorbed much of his time and he decided to hand over the business to his partners.

In 1929, as a sequence to his experiments with motion in still photography, Schuitema began work on a film. "The first revolutionary phase was over," says Schuitema. "Modern photography, modern typography, the modern film, the human document all came into existence during this period. I myself

Front page of a brochure for
Berkel weighing-machines

began to make documentary films. The practice of montage was vital to film-making. The possibilities of picture-making were extended beyond the confines of painting and the new means of pictorial expression were accepted everywhere. The camera took the place of the brush in the hands of the artist to depict documentary sketches and human documents. It was a quicker, simpler, more direct and more varied method of expression."

Again, as with still photography, Schuitema had to teach himself. Partly for economic reasons (but also because he was impatient to know what he had achieved) he developed and printed the films himself. His use of fine grain developer produced a broad tonal scale and enabled him to make good paper prints from the film negatives. But, on the other hand, his dense negatives gave much trouble to the laboratory that had later to make his final film copies.

Between 1929 and 1939 Schuitema made three films: *De Bruggen* (the bridges of Rotterdam), *De hallen* (the Paris food market, Les Halles) and *De Bouwhoek* (a country district in the province of Friesland in the north of Holland). Although he did not start working on all three at once, they were in fact simultaneously conceived as related explorations of movement. *De Bruggen* is concerned primarily with the movement of things; *De hallen* with the movement of people. In the third film, *De Bouwhoek,* it is the camera that moves over an unmoving land.

After the Second World War Schuitema made several further films, including *The Partisan's Song,* an experiment in the movement of colour. But since the death in 1953 of his close friend, Koos van de Grient (who composed the sound for *De Bruggen* and Schuitema's post-war films), Schuitema has made no further films.

Schuitema's career as a teacher began in 1930 when he became a lecturer at the Royal Academy in the Hague (where he continued to teach for thirty-three years). He encouraged his students to arrive at solutions through the exercise of reason and logic, and he demanded thoroughness and clarity in their work. His enthusiasm, his frankness and lack of pomp, and the exciting problems he posed his pupils, quickly established his reputation as a teacher.

Some of Schuitema's confident enthusiasm seems to have ebbed when he wrote, in 1961: "It is not easy to come to terms with the kind of world where one has to reckon with so many unknown factors. Artists tend to withdraw into themselves, to take refuge in abstraction, their relations with society have been destroyed and their whole activity is steeped in gloom." But then the old enthusiasm comes flooding back when he concludes: "We cannot recall it for it has already become part of history. The only possibility is to go on logically from there, from those clear, definite principles. Today the problem is more complicated. Men have not changed but circumstances have. It is nonsense to say that what happens is inevitable, but the shape of things can only be changed by great effort and it is always the individual who gives events a new direction. Western man must not yield, must not abandon the struggle. His strength lies not in physical force but in the powers of the mind. It is not a new romanticism which is needed but clarity of vision."

This indeed is the spirit that imbues Schuitema's work today. With typical thoroughness he has designed a colour reference system for printing. He has based this system on the colours used in the standard four-colour printing process. By dividing the halftone scale of each colour into an equal number of grades and numbering these from 0 to 9 he can refer to the halftone gradation in each of the four basic colours. Arranging these numbers as in their printing sequence, any cipher of four numbers relates to a colour in the system. The system covers a range of over 18,000 colours and provides a clear reference system for colour. Schuitema has also developed a simple method for revealing the relationship of different colours. Using a small number of master plates, each divided into ten rows of ten tones, and printing these in the normal four-colour order, a vast range of combinations results. Quite apart from the usefulness of this system in printing, the reference prints, developed by pure reason, are themselves of unexpected and exceptional beauty.

Herbert Spencer
in conversation

London, 22 August, 1980

Fletcher Can you tell us something of why and how you began your professional career?

Spencer I became passionately interested in printing at the age of twelve. I don't remember what sparked it off, or why printing had this extraordinary fascination for me which still exists.

My keen interest in printing lasted for several years, but in my mid-teens during the early years of the war, I gravitated much more towards painting and drawing. This had become a very strong preoccupation by the time I volunteered for the Air Force. But while I was waiting to be called up I got a job with Cecil B Notley, the advertising agent. There, at the age of seventeen and a half, I realized that my knowledge of type was really quite an asset. I found that I had stumbled on a profession in which I could function.

After I came out of the Air Force, I needed to get some sort of job to support myself, and it was then that I met Leon French and William Morgan. They were trained compositors who had worked as typographical designers at the Ministry of Information during the war, and had now formed a small group called London Typographical Designers. I joined them.

LTD designed a lot of technical catalogues, as well as brochures and a certain amount of press advertising. It was all fairly prestigious stuff, and some of the publications were highly complex.

Sometime later something happened which made it seem possible for me to break away. I was approached by the director of the Linguists' Club in Grosvenor Place to redesign all their printed material, including a monthly magazine.

There was undoubtedly a tremendous element of chance in my career up to the age of twenty-four, because if something else had come along at any stage, I might easily have moved in some quite other direction. However, about this time a number of things seemed to fall into place.

Fletcher I still remember an invitation card done by Max Huber in the early 1950s, and suppose that as a student I was very impressed with the design. Is there a similar piece of typographic work which sticks in your mind?

Spencer During the early 1940s I remember being struck by some of

64

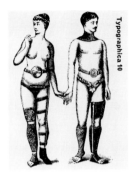

Typographica 10

Tschichold's work reproduced in Robert Harling's excellent pre-war journal *Typography,* of which, sadly, only eight issues appeared. In particular I remember an advertisement he had designed for Paul Graupe "Auktion 105". Just after the war, when I began to get really seriously interested in typography, I remember also being much impressed by Max Bill's 1947 *Allianz* catalogue cover for the Kunsthaus Zurich.

Apart from these individual pieces of work which have stuck in my mind, I think two books I bought when I was about sixteen had a great influence on my ideas.

Someone had given me a present of Vincent Steer's massive volume on typography but I really didn't think much of that. And I remember selling it for a pound in Charing Cross Road and then I went next door to Zwemmer's and bought the Bauhaus book for, I believe, one guinea. I found it tremendously exciting. Another thing I bought second-hand about the same time was Alfred Barr's Museum of Modern Art book called *Cubism and Abstract Art,* which had been published some years earlier in 1936. This set many of the works towards which I felt attracted in design, architecture, painting and sculpture in a broader perspective and made comprehensible to me many of the movements and ideas that were then current.

Fletcher Looking back, I can focus on certain contemporary designers who have influenced my attitudes to typography, for example, Paul Rand. Can you tell us something about similar influences in your career?

Spencer In my early twenties I found the work being done by Sandberg in Holland, Pierre Faucheux in France and Max Huber in Italy very stimulating, particularly in the use of different materials which seemed to give some of their work a three-dimensional quality.

I was also moved by the prints of H N Werkman, the Dutch printer-painter who had been executed on almost the last day of the German occupation of Holland. Werkman is certainly someone I would strongly advise any student to look at seriously and enjoy. Indeed, he and most of the other twentieth-century designers I consider important are included in my book *Pioneers of Modern Typography.*

Fletcher Is there any single piece of typography you have done of which you feel particularly fond?

Spencer Of my various publications I think *Pioneers* is perhaps the one of most lasting value, although *The Visible Word* and the much earlier *Design in Business Printing* (which was the result of my teaching experience at the Central School) were important at the time they were published. But it is certainly *Typographica* for which I have the deepest affection and for which, perhaps, I shall be best remembered.

Fletcher I much regret the demise of *Typographica* magazine. Was this due to economics, or your difficulty in maintaining articles of interest?

Spencer *Typographica* was, of course, a marvellous thing to do and I am terribly glad I started it when I did. Looking back I am amazed to find that I was able to keep it going eighteen years. But I think there is a right time to end activities as well as to start them and I do not regret bringing *Typographica* to an end when I did – although I do regret, and am greatly surprised, that no young and enthusiastic person has stepped in to produce something comparable since.

Fletcher I am regularly surprised at most design students' ignorance, even lack of curiosity, of the major influences in the field in which they profess to be studying. What is your reaction to this comment as professor at the Royal College of Art?

Spencer What you say is sadly true. I am sometimes depressed when interviewing candidates for the College, not only by their ignorance of their chosen subject, but also their uncritical attitude and general lack of interest in the cultural life of their time.

Fletcher I assume you have some criteria in mind when suggesting certain work or publications which you feel a student could learn from?

Spencer The important thing in typographic design is of course the content, and the designer is, or should be, the bridge between the author and the reader. This does not mean that typography should be dull or invisible. But it does mean that the bridge should not peter out halfway across the ravine. A printed text is not just texture on the page: it is the vehicle for conveying information or the author's ideas and emotions.

Fletcher If asked to produce a Spencer exhibition of only ten pieces, which would they be and why?

Spencer Although many of my commissions give me enormous pleasure at the time, there are few pieces of work (other than *Typographica*) for which I feel particularly enthusiastic in the long term, and I certainly would not consider putting on an exhibition of only ten pieces, as you suggest. As I explained in an interview published in the *Designer* (the SIA journal), I am really against the idea of treating typography as a means for creating paper monuments.

BRUNO MONGUZZI

Italy

Piet Zwart:
the typographical work 1923-33

Rassegna, 30/2, Milan, 1987

I t was while collaborating with the architect Jan Wils that Piet Zwart turned himself into a typographer in order to design Wils' personal stationery around a geometric symbol – a small square outlined by five bars – which Wils had stamped on his plans since 1916. It was Wils himself who introduced Zwart to the Dutch representative of Vickers House, the English rubber flooring manufacturer. Almost by accident, Zwart's typographical career started in this way in 1921. He designed commercial materials, some cards, a poster and later a large billboard for Vickers House. For the *Loco* logotype and for the design of some large lettering, he used (as Huszar and Van Doesburg had also obsessively done) a grid of squares that he quickly abandoned because of its resemblance to the anti-classical but nonetheless ornamental typographical work that Wijdeveld had introduced in 1918 in the magazine *Wendignen*. "When I started my typographical work Wijdeveld was the number one man. Only later did I realize that my way of doing things was a protest against the spirit of the times. I didn't consider Wijdeveld a reactionary: his work was the expression of that period; he was part of an old technical world with its old methods. We, on the other hand, tried to give a concrete basis to the ideas of the avant-garde – an avant-garde that had started well before the World War. The universal Exhibition in London in 1851 could be considered as the starting point. It demonstrated how a man's product is largely determined by the technology available to him."

Vickers House, Den Haag,
card c.1923

At the beginning of 1923, Berlage introduced Zwart to his son-in-law, a manager of NKF, Nederlandse Kabelfabriek in Delft, and thus began their ten-year-long collaboration.

Despite his occasional prior graphic experience, Zwart started out completely lacking typographical skills. "I did my first advertisement completely in Indian ink, but since the magazine it was supposed to appear in came out before I finished my design, I understood that that was not the right method. I learned principles of typography from an eighteen-year-old apprentice in a little print shop; during the lunch hour, I showed him my sketches and together we tried to set them in metal type. I started without the slightest idea of what typography was; I didn't even know the

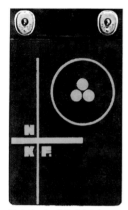

Nederlandse Kabelfabriek,
Delft, catalogue front cover,
bound with snaps for updating
summaries. 1924.

meaning of the terms "upper and lower case" or "capital".

In January, at Huszar's, Zwart met Kurt Schwitters who was in Holland for the famous Dada campaign in which he participated with his wife, Helma, Theo and Nelly Van Doesburg, and Huszar himself. Zwart talked about it with Kees Broos in 1968: "Wonderful meetings, incredible confusion... The first evening in the Oude Doelen in Rotterdam, there was a fight and the second the police were there in force. Tremendous! Punches! Blood! That Schwitters was great; he was completely unperturbed; quite the opposite of Van Doesburg. In tails, his silk cape, top-hat, ha ha, a good man, you know!... I don't think he was such a great graphic artist, but he was a fantastic man of letters and his *Merzbilder* were beautiful."

Zwart's incipient typographical work found new dynamic expression, initially close to Dadaist exuberance and later more and more constructive. This occurred in concomitance with the first issues of *Merz* (in issue no. 4, Schwitters published Lissitzky's brief manifesto on typography), together with his important meeting with Lissitzky around the middle of May. On 18 May, Lissitzky gave a lecture at the Art Circle in The Hague on "new Russian art" in which he said: "Artists must organize their ranks; they must build a party. It's wrong to think the things learned through school are a means for the expression of personal freedom, but rather our own philosophy. Today, anyone who wants to create something must first mould a new consciousness; anyone who wants to participate in the process of creation of the new culture must study the elements of current experience. Only then will he reach new goals and affirm them in life through the organization of a party. Because life does not recognize any isolated figure."

Lissitzky gave Zwart a copy with a dedication in it of *Dlya Golossa* (For the Voice), thirteen poems written by Mayakovsky, and meant to be read aloud. The book was edited by Lily Brik, and Lissitzky had just "constructed" and printed it in Berlin for Moscow's State Editions, using almost exclusively material from the type case. At the time Zwart already owned no. 42 of the 50 signed copies of *Two Squares*, the Dutch version of *Pro Dva Kvadrata* published a few months before as issue no. 10/11 of *De Stijl*. Lissitzky also showed Zwart (who knew nothing about photography) how to directly fix photographic shadows on sensitized paper without using a negative.

The impact that this meeting with Lissitzky had on Zwart's work became evident in his subsequent advertisements and in the small 1924 catalogue-diary he did for NKF, in which his first photogram appeared – the first photogram, along with Lissitzky's famous Pelikan bottle, ever used in advertising. In this small notebook, put together with two snaps in order to make it possible to update the technical summaries in the appendix which was sent out annually with a calendar card, Zwart used the idea of the index

Nederlandse Kabelfabriek,
Delft, advertisement, 1924

that Lissitzky had introduced in *For the Voice* to allow the "reciter to find individual poems more quickly".

In the first advertisement that Zwart planned for the telephone wires in January 1924, in order to denote each one of the four cities, Paris, London, Vienna and Berlin, he designed a full disc inside a thin circular crown (clichés that he would use several times) just as Lissitzky had already done for London, Paris and Berlin next to the poem, *Scoundrels!* To make the large letters or numbers that he used as structural elements and also as surprising centres of interest, which he often counterposed to small body sizes, Zwart almost always used lines, bars, corners and squares that he found in the type case.

Between 1923 and 1933, the year in which he ended his collaboration with Nederlandse Kabelfabriek due to an economic disagreement, Zwart designed slightly fewer than 300 advertisements that came out regularly, first in the monthly *Tijdschrift voor electrotechniek* and then in the biweekly *Sterkstroom*, both published in The Hague. These ads were almost exclusively typographical, with the exception of the last ones in which he cropped and fogged his photographs, in some of which he introduced a sectioned line, and a couple from 1924-5 in which he re-used photograms already created for the small catalogue-diary. These advertisements demonstrated his consistent ability to express in visual terms any peculiarity present in the concise texts that he himself wrote. He visually enhanced anaphoras, assonance and alliteration, emphasized the same stroke in different letters as a structural sign for the rhythmic scanning of the background, obsessively repeated words or phrases until they became surface, texture or hyperbole. The asymmetrical distribution of the elements, which in the beginning were strongly heterogeneous in body size, weight and typeface (starting in 1929, though, he consistently used only one typeface, all lower case), the increasingly sharpened introduction of the diagonal, the large empty backgrounds where white played an active role in the compositional process, and the recurring invention of discordant signs (which Zwart meaningfully called "eye-catchings") caused these advertisements to systematically emerge from their typographical context. For the first time, the poetic tradition that originated in the attempt to give verse a visual form corresponding to the verbal rhythm was extended to a utilitarian sphere. It was Mallarmé with his poem, *Un Coup de dés jamais n'abolira le hasard*, who first marked out this path; later it was followed by Apollinaire in *Calligrammes* and Marinetti in *Parole in libertà*, and by the Dadaists Huelsenbeck, Janco and Tzara in *L'admiral cherche une maison à louer* and Van Doesburg, who started publishing his *X-beelden* in *De Stijl* under the pseudonym JK Bonset in May 1920. The "De Stijl" group's second manifesto, *Literature*, which appeared in the April

1920 issue, read: "The word must be reconstructed by following the sound as well as the idea." It continued, "duality between form and content cannot exist." Lissitzky, too, in his "Typographical Facts", which appeared in *Writings in Honour of Gutenberg* in Mainz in 1925, talked at length about the correlation: "Language is something more than the simple movement of acoustic waves or purely a means for the transmission of thought. Typography is also something more than simple movement of optic waves with the same purpose... Therefore, plastic typography must do for optics what the orator's voice and gestures do for the expression of his thoughts."

The plan is thus to break down the closed structure of traditional typography by opening it up to the rhythmic-dynamic requirements of the text. But for Zwart it was a question of also freeing the reader from the enslaving monotony of reading caused by typographical rules. Zwart wanted his reader to immediately reach his goal; he had to be able to easily distinguish between what was fundamental and what was secondary, what he wanted to read from what he wanted to leave out. Just as a Parisian critic in 1926 would baptize a restaurant designed by Zwart "Ford à manger", once more paraphrasing Le Corbusier, Dr Jaffe would view Zwartian typography in retrospect as "*une machine à lire*". "These advertising ideas have nothing to do with art," Zwart said. "They are just *objective* products in which the attempt has been made to have typography work with the advertising concept as a coherent *result*." A selection of these "ephemeral prints", as he called them, was shown at the International Exhibition of decorative and modern industrial arts in Paris in 1925...

Drukkerij Trio, Den Haag, cover, 1931

In 1930, Zwart designed a promotional catalogue for the Trio co-operative, his usual printer, on the occasion of the expansion of the company. The catalogue, although it reached the advanced stages, was never printed. It included a brief essay, "From the old to the new typography", in which Zwart, after a detailed historic digression, explained his typographical credo: "Even typography undergoes changes: its range of activity has expanded enormously. In addition to books, it produces newspapers, magazines, documents, advertising. New publications reach us daily. It is one of the most active means for the development and advancement of the people; in effect, it is typography that makes the creation of mass culture possible.... Power in the service of society; to perform this task, it must adapt its form to the spirit of our times.... While the old typography was arranged symmetrically (the lines were lined up with respect to the page's central axis and this layout was maintained even at the expense of logic), the new typography sets the lines with ragged edge aligning them up on the left and then letting them end where they may, or by controlling the line breaks to cause a certain tension in the text (that is what happens in advertising). The new typography, then, in the normal function of reading, appears asymmetrical. The new typography is functional; the old was decorative. It not only decorated with ornaments, flourishes and vignettes, but also through the combination of multiple characters. The new typography, as the importance of reading demands, uses functional characters. It doesn't need ornaments. It also does away with the apparently innocent residues of the pleasure of ornamenting, such as bars and circles, if they do not have any function.... The new typography is elementary. It negates any pre-established formal plan; it subordinates form to function; it constructs the page with black and white in such a way as to affirm the tensions of the text.... Today, we want more objective type; advertising requires an aggressive legibility. The 'Sanserif' seems to best meet these requirements, but only for the moment, since its form is certainly not ideal. Although there is an insane, unlimited multiplication of types of letters, variations and 'improvements', an elementary typeface that establishes its functionality on scientific bases has not yet been designed.... The new typography has to be content with the most simple, least ornate and most rational typefaces. In any event, those faces with a high-handed, personal, idiosyncratic seal should be avoided; their pretentious character opposes the utilitarian task of typography. The more uninteresting a letter is in itself the more useful it is in typography. A typeface is interesting when it is free of historicist vestiges and expresses the exact spirit of the twentieth century. Every period has its own typical typographic character. Ours has yet to find it. These signs must be based on the needs of optic physiology, not on individualistic considerations and preferences.... Modern man's critical spirit distinguishes the superfluous, the uneconomical and the subjective from the essential, and tends towards new expressive forms in order to reach new solutions and new possibilities for use; man tries to approach maximum feasibility, utility and efficiency. The modern typographer who starts to reflect on these elements trips over his own alphabet. He wonders why there are four signs for one sound, why *TtTt, DdDd, AaAa*, if only two are necessary in the case.... There is no plausible reason why a line should begin with a capital letter; no one, except for the Germans, finds it necessary to start nouns with a capital... Holland is as arbitrary as hOLLAND.... The old typography operated on a two-dimensional plane – static; when it used xylography or other forms of illustration, it considered them in a decorative sense and not as an integral part of the entire composition process. The use of photography (photograms and photomontages included) as an integral element in composition makes the new typography three-dimensional – dynamic. Space and movement are incorporated into its field of activity."

According to Zwart, the active element of composition was

Drukkerij Trio, Den Haag, inside page, 1931

BRUNO MONGUZZI

located precisely in the conflict between these two factors, the three-dimensionality of the image and the two-dimensionality of the text. He concluded his essay by asserting that while the old typography was "contemplative, imitative, decorative and individual," the new typography had to be "actively effective, plastically expressive, elementarily functional and collective".

These two extracts are taken from a much longer study of the work of the Dutch designer Piet Zwart (1885-1977). Zwart was connected with members of the "De Stijl" group, such as the painter Vilmos Huszar, and in the 1920s worked in the office of Hendrik Berlage, who was an enthusiast for the work of Frank Lloyd Wright and who influenced the architects of the "De Stijl" group. For fourteen years Zwart taught the history of art at the Rotterdam Academy, interpreting works of art in their broadest social context and adding a course in technical design similar in style to the Bauhaus preparatory course. Among his creative friendships were those with Schwitters, Tschichold and Schuitema. His typographical work is a major aspect of his fertile and unconventional career.

CHAPTER 2

Design Education

Félix Beltrán
Armin Hofmann
Burton Kramer
Mervyn Kurlansky
Katherine McCoy
Jan Rajlich
Deborah Sussman

FÉLIX BELTRÁN

Mexico

The Bauhaus vision

**Lecture: Homage to the 50th Anniversary of the Bauhaus,
National Library, Havana, 1969**

The famous and controversial Bauhaus was established in 1919 in Weimar by Walter Gropius as the School of Architecture and Applied Art, the merger of the two most important art institutions of Saxony: the Sächsische Hochschule für Bildende Kunst and the Kunstgewerbeschule. It became the most important hub for European arts after World War 1. The Bauhaus's didactic ideals constituted a transcendental effort to overcome the crisis in modern art by linking the art of industrial production to the specific needs of society.

The school moved to Dessau in 1925, where Walter Gropius designed a comfortable school building that remains one of the main examples of rationalism in architecture. Gropius himself was director of the Bauhaus until 1928, succeeded by Hannes Meyer who was expelled by the Social Democrats in 1930. The school moved to Berlin where Ludwig Mies van der Rohe was the director in 1933, the year in which the Nazis closed down the school because of its democratic ideals and experimentation with modern art.

In the development of the Bauhaus, one may identify two stages: the mystic-expressionist, corresponding to the Weimar period, which influenced its teaching methods, and the Dessau period, characterized by constructivism of the "industrial aesthetics", which proposed elementary constants through the use of basic media. This pursuit of drastic reductionism would result in "pure forms". The latter was conditioned by its relationship with and differences from the Dutch movement of De Stijl, in particular through Theo van Doesburg, whom Walter Gropius never allowed into the school.

"The ultimate goal of every plastic activity is construction. To serve as an ornament to construction was, in certain periods, the most important task of the other plastic arts, which were then inseparable components of architecture. Today, painting, sculpture, and architecture are each in a state of self-sufficient individualism, from which they can free themselves only through the joint, conscious, and coordinated actions of all artists.... The old schools of art were incapable of creating this unity.... We, architects, sculptors, painters, must return to the crafts, because in fact there

74

is no professional art.... There is no essential difference between artist and artisan.... Together, let us conceive, invent, create the new structure of the future, one that encompasses all in one: architecture, sculpture, painting; one built by millions of artisans' hands, which will rise someday toward heaven as a clear symbol of a new, future faith."

Those ideals were stated by Gropius for the Weimar Bauhaus, a school whose prominent faculty included Lyonel Feininger, Johannes Itten, and Gerhardt Marcks. The founding of the Bauhaus coincided with the economic crisis that affected a defeated Germany after World War 1. Although only industry could promote economic recovery, industry was also seen as the cause of the war and the subsequent disaster. The Bauhaus vision emerges from the realization that there was an urgent need to rectify the mistakes that had made industry a destructive force. Industry as a constructive force became the goal. To do so, art and crafts had to be linked to economic production, as had been the case throughout history until the advent of the Industrial Revolution, when art became separated from the workcycle. Critics such as John Ruskin and William Morris pointed out how industry, in spite of established values, had accepted a deficient aesthetic presence in the products.

The Bauhaus adopted the postulates of the German movement Werkbund which had proposed the coming together of the artist and industrial production to create prototypes that the industrial process could mass produce. To the Bauhaus, the goal was to produce objects that would carry the new industrial aesthetics by means of the new didactics the Bauhaus espoused. The artist/artisan was to become part of the cycle of production of "prophetic" objects. It was hoped that art would be present in all everyday activities and circumstances. Art would produce useful objects, identical for all and perfectly functional, so that society could be conscious of its unity and of its commitment to a common effort for the future.

Also influential in the Dessau period was Russian Constructivism, especially the ideas of the Vkhutemas, the School of Advanced Technical and Artistic Studies, established in Moscow a year before the Bauhaus. The Vkhutemas had Kasimir Malevich, Antoine Pevsner, El Lissitzky, Vladimir Tatlin, and Wassily Kandinsky (who later went to the Bauhaus) among its teachers. The Vkhutemas also defended the new industrial aesthetics and opposed the cosmopolitanism of the School of Paris, the latter characterized by loyalty to the artists' personality. At the Bauhaus, the artist specialized in the industrial process. His activity was related to urbanism which greatly determines the living conditions of the community and the architecture, and with all industrially produced objects. Standards were essential in order to attain unity in a society's habits and to incorporate the individual into a collective order.

As to Bauhaus curriculum, the initial Vorkurs course was

75

launched by Johannes Itten, bearer of the new didactics. He was influenced by August Frobel, who believed learning had to be approached as a game. Itten's teaching methods, centred on the exaltation of the student's individual talents and his potential capabilities, required that the student learn to relax, to breathe, and to concentrate, as essential steps to be taken before proceeding to intensive labour. The psychophysical phase of teaching was followed by the didactic part. Itten discussed forms and colours and presented them in every possible polar contrast. Then he proceeded to the intellectual contents: straight/curved, dark/light, hard/soft, while making reference to colour contrast and spatial dimensions. Presenting these contrasts separately or in different relationships allowed the senses to capture them. Itten's method refers to the three ways to consider form and colour: in terms of quality and quantity; in terms of how they are recognized by the senses, and in terms of how they are perceived by the intellect and emotions.

The Bauhaus, Dessau, designed by Walter Gropius. View from south-east wing, 1925

Another component of Itten's didactics included the meticulous study of the natural world and the analysis of the properties of different materials, as well as the representation of existing forms, including the analysis of the works of early artists.

The tendency toward representation would later be diminished by the influence of abstract art. "To delve deeply into and to control the experiences," said Johannes Itten, "it is necessary to touch, look and depict these textures until they are known totally, so as to depict them outside their natural model, from one's own interior experiences." His didactic clearly shows a mimetic tendency not oriented in the traditional way, but in the search for thorough knowledge of the materials' properties. It is possible then to understand how the mystic-expressionist orientation of Johannes Itten had to disappear when faced with the constructivist tendency that was growing in the Bauhaus. In 1922, the preliminary course passed into the hands of Georg Muche and months later, Johannes Itten abandoned the Bauhaus. He was succeeded by the artist Laszlo Moholy-Nagy, who, like Josef Albers, was an artist turned teacher. He was responsible for the analysis of existing forms, as well as mathematics, biotechniques and the analysis of new forms and their properties. To bring materials to his classes was his main contribution. Josef Albers was responsible for the analysis of materials, especially paper. Through folding and free experimentation, paper offered infinite possibilities for new forms exempt from functional use. The results were critiqued by teachers and pupils. In this respect, his didactics were oriented toward the study of techniques. According to Josef Albers, technique serves to discover the internal forces and practical possibilities of the materials and to produce more impersonal structures, from collages to montages.

A sense of economy was an essential facet of his didactics, to instil in his pupils the idea that from a minimum of elements, one should reach maximum efficiency in the results. One of his oft-repeated concepts was that a work is good when nothing is left over. The analysis of visual illusions as part of the experiments was, at the same time, another basic element of his didactics. In contrast to Johannes Itten, Josef Albers saw in randomness a sense of irresponsibility. "When calculations fail, randomness intervenes: that is irresponsibility."

In 1928, at the suggestion of Walter Gropius, another architect, Hannes Meyer, succeeded him as the director of the Bauhaus. He added to the curriculum new disciplines, such as political economics. To Hannes Meyer, the Bauhaus had to aspire to real practical works for real environments. During this time, Josef Albers continued to direct the preliminary course. In 1930 the Social Democratic authorities expelled Hannes Meyer from the Bauhaus, as a result of his "Marxist orientation, contrary to the standing concepts about architecture and corruptive of youth." The main reason for his expulsion was a donation he made to the miners of Mansfield. The Bauhaus was raided and the foreign teachers were deported.

Before leaving for Moscow, Hannes Meyer told the press that his trip "is to work in that country where a truly proletarian culture is being forged, where socialism is being born, where a society that we in Dessau fought for under capitalism, already exists."

After the departure of Hannes Meyer, the Bauhaus was reopened in Berlin under the direction of the architect Ludwig Mies van der Rohe. In spite of adverse circumstances, it kept some of its teachers and pupils. But in this final stage of the Bauhaus, the preliminary course had the effect of levelling, according to common precepts, the differences among the students with regard to previous concepts and attitudes. That had never happened before.

In 1933, the Bauhaus was closed down by the Nazis, accused of being a centre of Bolshevik culture.

ARMIN HOFMANN

Switzerland

Between progress and art

Graphis, Nr. 287, Zürich, September/October 1993

Design is clearly not a priority in our school system at present. From elementary and intermediate through high school, arts courses rank fairly low on the curriculum. And even in this outsider position, art education is further devalued by the minor role that art plays in the grades that appear on a student's report card. Art's emotional, sensory approach to thinking is considered the exact opposite of intellectual, pragmatic reasoning, which is valued much more highly. Modes of working that emphasize deeper, more complex, but also livelier forms of perception are probably difficult to integrate into an educational model predicated on functional, rational thought.

Although there are current reform efforts, they merely aim at an improved co-ordination within the existing curriculum while leaving the old priorities intact. They are about a more relaxed learning environment, new ways of teaching and the advancement of comprehensive training. Yet they barely begin to touch the traditional top-heaviness of the entire system. Apparently there are fears that an emphasized, more integrated art education in grade schools could lead to more than a clash of opposing teaching principles. Quite likely it is the opposing philosophies behind the two teaching objectives that cause anxiety in school officials and politicians.

But also in the public's mind, arts-related subjects are still widely relegated to the realm of superfluous and eccentric. If art could finally be rescued from isolation, if art and creative work could again be understood as everyday activities, artistic subjects might effortlessly be integrated into the curriculum as part of an important social task. Any honest effort, any job that is carried out with dedication and joy, is ultimately the beginning of an artistic mode of behaviour. The fact that artistic subjects, due to their flexible structure, can serve as models for more unwieldy disciplines has barely been recognized. Equally surprising is the lack of positive response by schools and the public to modern, early twentieth-century painting, whose goals included exploring and exposing the forces behind visual design.

From grade school on, a clear demarcation line prevents

interconnected, interdependent parts appearing as a whole. The necessary interaction between functional, pragmatic thinking and lively quest for inner truths is thus cut off. Strictly speaking, it is impossible to genuinely grasp any subject without an inner, spiritual approach. Only a comprehensive educational approach on general artistic principles can provide the kind of experiences that transcend accumulated technical knowledge. No matter how one defines art, artistic creation or artistic learning, no other field applies the humanistic principles of a comprehensive education as directly. Only when intellect and artistic experience, purposefulness and leisure, certainty and intuition can interact as complements will there be a platform on which creative behaviour can develop.

The result of all this is that design schools, with their mission of fostering creative thinking and imaginative action, must build their programmes on weak foundations. Besides the increasingly difficult task of familiarizing students with new forms of thinking and working at a relatively late stage in their lives, design schools exist in an environment that is none too favourable for them. More and more they feel like alien elements in an economically driven society that appears increasingly devoted to the measurable, concrete shape of things.

But even in their own mission, design schools have begun to falter. Under pressure from a *Zeitgeist* beholden to technological progress they cannot help but upgrade their tools to what is currently the state of the art. High-tech equipment, new media, advanced reproduction and production methods have given the old arts and crafts schools a new look but also new challenges. Every day, teachers and students are confronted with new forms and content generated by modern means of communication. To an ever increasing extent, technological realities call into question the value of the traditional basic subjects, i.e. drawing, colour, typography, etc. Are these subjects still adequate means of providing the artistic intelligence with new perspectives that go beyond pure aesthetics?

The answer to this question will determine the future development of our design schools – and whether they will be able to fulfil their cultural task in a modern society. In almost all design schools the basic courses have been cut back and are taught in such a perfunctory manner that they have ceased to give any genuine fundamental training. There is an obvious danger that the new *Zeitgeist* in our design schools will soon be limited to supplying copy machines, computers, printers, cameras, film and video equipment without providing concepts for using them in a meaningful way. It is no secret that these new tools not only affect the form of information but also influence its contents.

Every design school has the responsibility of exploring this interplay between man and technology because the positive

79

energies generated by the new equipment come in tandem with serious negative forces, which have a particularly strong impact on the field of applied visual design.

Art and design schools, especially the departments dealing with communication issues, are more directly affected by the current technological changes than any other institutions of learning. Indeed, these changes go to their very core. Today they are obliged to grapple with the technologically driven world of machines as much as they do the realm of feeling and imagination. Since visual representation functions as a vernacular that must fulfil general communication tasks, design schools are challenged to tackle issues such as meaning, production and transmission of images. The implicit job of interlinking artistic work with media-specific realities is now confronting them with problems that are quite novel in their complexity. Consequently, one of the schools' most important tasks will be to unite human methods with conditions prescribed by new technological media. This means that they need to revise their basic artistic training by emphasizing a deeper spiritual understanding and by refuting the present tendency toward objectification. Basic training gains a heightened importance in today's altered conditions, but it is quite obvious that the substance of basic artistic training has become too feeble to support the professional superstructure that increasingly deals with technological processes.

There are examples everywhere: magazines and other publications in which the relationship between picture, text and colour has been lost. A surfeit of colour that is largely determined by electronics, repetitive in its uniform brightness and employed as a mere stimulant. A gratuitously arranged accumulation of studio photographs, battle shots, scientific pictures, etc., which in the absence of any meaningful context devalues and trivializes the documented events.

Several factors contribute to the deplorable state of our visual culture. But in a society that has come to rely so heavily on visual information, the schools, from grade school through to university, have a responsibility to find new forms of communication that can serve as a basis for social intercourse.

BURTON KRAMER

Canada

The hunger

White Space, Ontario College of Art, 1988-89

W hat is the flavour of Cerulean Blue? Or Cobalt Blue? Or Pantone Reflex Blue? And does that flavour somehow connect with "Blue is for Boys", "Singing the Blues", "Blue Skies (Fair Weather)", "The Blue-bird of Happiness"? What does blue icing (on the cake) really taste like? Is it mint? No, that's green.

When we consider using the colour blue, do some/all of the above come to mind? Always/never? How much Tobasco (red) do we need to add to get a warm (hot?) blue... before it becomes, oh my God – purple?

Proust reminds us that we depend strongly on, and remember with, our sense of smell. The CNE? The races? The beach? What is that you're wearing? Mmmm! Bumper to bumper (exhaust fumes are so tasty) to/from the cottage, the office. Can we separate taste from smell?

What sort of form looks "yummy", or friendly, if not downright affectionate? Can we establish clear connections with "natural" forms? What sort of form looks serious, honest, believable? What forms look rebellious, nervous, dangerous, aggressive, hostile, warlike, scary?

How did the whirling sun (symbol of energy, of life-giving) become a form of dread – the swastika? Clearly, our reaction to any form is modified (sometimes considerably) by the ways in which it relates to our storehouse of associations, parallels and connections.

Do we see with our eyes? More likely with our eyes, ears, nose, sense of touch, and even taste – with a complex combination of all our senses. Even the intervals, the pauses, the "negative" spaces between the pulsed messages play a continuous and major role.

And how do we really see? To begin with, we have to "pay attention". This implies focus, concentration. And like a lens set to a wide f-stop at close range, when we "focus" on a detail, most of the background becomes unfocused. We focus, then, on "bits", like parts of a dark room seen by the narrow beam of a penlight. Whatever we know, through past experience, enables us to conjure up for ourselves some image of the room. But that image will depend on what bits of the room our penlight happened to

81

illuminate, and on what we think we saw.

This constant necessity to create a totality from perceived bits is an expression of our need to make connections and understand our relationship to everything around us. Without this process, we'd be truly lost at sea, trying desperately to see, unable to put things together.

The possible connections become more complex as you read, listen, and taste a lot of things over a period of time. Books, music, theatre, art, theory, philosophy, religion, architecture, design, sports, travel, love. The associations, the parallels are yours, enabling you to cook up dishes that may seem old, but are new again through you. You've added some magic ingredients!

The best designers, artists, musicians, dancers, writers and cooks all have "The Hunger". Remember Catherine Deneuve as a 2,000-year-old (gorgeous) vampire? Always hungry! Insatiable! Or the lines from Brecht, "What keeps a man alive? He lives on others. He tastes them first, then swallows them whole." Food may be fuel, or energy, or learning.

Designers and other creative (hungry) types are interested in a varied menu which may include toys, African sculpture, Pre-Columbian art and artifacts, Indonesian masks, puzzles, music, letterforms, signs, dolls, Molas, magazines, books, and more books, attempting through all of them to find out what's happening, to learn how it all got to be this way. And through this on-going learning process the designer who knows a little bit about a lot of things will begin to put it all together, to draw the parallels and make the connections.

Doing this and doing it well is to be a great chef, a master musician, an important film-maker, a tribal magician, a generalist... a real person!

It takes generalists in this time of specialization (and designers, "real" designers are generalists) to absorb everything they can, and having done so, be capable of cooking up Tasty Dishes for Every Occasion.

MERVYN KURLANSKY

Denmark

Masking is revealing

Danmarks Designskole, autumn 1991

I f you ever visit Pentragram's design studio in London, look out for an unusual collection of primitive masks on the wall of the reception area. Collecting masks has been an abiding interest of the Pentagram design partners for a long time. Theo Crosby started it all some years ago and the rest of us have carried on the tradition.

For Theo's sixtieth birthday, sixty architects, artists and designers were each asked to create a mask as a gift, so the collection has grown. But why are we, as designers, so interested in the culture and traditions of mask-making? And what significance does it have to the modern ritual of designing for the printed medium?

These were the questions at the heart of a two-day workshop which I ran at the Danmarks Designskole for graphic design students.

Each student was asked to create a mask which made a statement about his or her individual personality and creative approach.

The results of the workshop were stunning in the way the masks revealed personal character and made a statement about individual influences, memories and emotions.

In modern European culture, the mask has come to symbolize disguise or protection so that true identity and feelings can be hidden. But if you look at the ancient origins of mask-making and its continuing importance in primitive African societies, then the mask has a spiritual significance which is self-revelatory. The wearing of the mask unmasks the wearer. The African mask holds the key to much of our understanding of the way mask-making is at the root of psychological behaviour. According to Andreas Lommel, author of *Masks: Their Meaning and Function* (Paul Elek Books, l972), the African mask is "more than mere disguise, for it gives expression to the bond between a group of people and their ancestors. At the same time a mask is the embodiment of a tradition and a guarantee of the continuity of an order hallowed by tradition."

Masks in African societies play a myriad roles, which have been the subject of analysis by cultural historians. Masks have been used for centuries in dances and rituals to celebrate harvests, guard crops, initiate boys into manhood, worship ancestors, confirm social order, exorcise evil spirits, frighten off mortal enemies and provide entertainment, often of a frivolous and caricaturing nature. The wearer of the mask takes on the divine spirit so the design and artistry of the mask is linked to the spirit world.

"Within African art, the aspect of the face has strict iconographic meaning. Both masks and figures are reliquaries of divine power, whether their function is intended to be profound, or frivolous or entertaining," explains Robert Bleakley, writing in *African Masks* (Thames and Hudson, 1978). He adds that masks must be "either as beautiful or as terrifying as possible in order for the spirit to choose to inhabit them."

If the mask gives the African tribesman the power and confidence to perform in a special and different way, so revealing inner beliefs and motivations, then the same principle holds true in modern societies.

I recall visiting the Swiss spring festival of Fassnacht, a three-day carnival, and being amazed to see the normally rational and conservative Swiss adorn themselves with masks and costumes and really let their hair down.

If I think back to my earliest experiences with masks and costumes, then they were in a way revealing about me. I grew up in South Africa and remember an invitation to my first masquerade. My family were not wealthy enough to buy an entire costume so I swathed myself in old bandages and daubed myself with tomato sauce. My improvised costume gave me the courage to behave in a way I wouldn't have dared if people had known who I really was.

The same was true on my first voyage to England. For a fancy dress party, I became a bare-chested pirate complete with eye-patch and sword borrowed from a fencing team on board the ship. I behaved outrageously. Obviously I didn't believe in the spiritual magic of the mask in the same way as the African or Polynesian tribesman. But although the supernatural power of the mask may have been eroded in our minds, it can still act as a catalyst for sudden changes in human behaviour. Psychological studies of revellers at the Rio Carnival have proved that.

Some of the original significance of the mask survives in its modern use in theatre or sports. From the Japanese Noh plays to the *Phantom of the Opera*, the mask has remained at the heart of the dramatic revelation. From the ferocious headgear of the intimidating American footballer to the victorious masked wrestler who refuses to reveal his true identity to his opponent, the mask plays tricks with who we are and what we think we are. These are some of the ideas that we explored in the Danmarks Designskole mask workshop. The students were given a day-and-a-half to devise their individual masks. They worked hard and they worked fast. They used a variety of materials – some moulded papier mâché, others pressed wire to their faces. They explored a variety of ideas and emotions. There was a lot of soul-searching and a lot of fun. The solutions

84

were abstract, animalistic, artful.

One student decided to expess his feelings about his father, who was interested in music and photography. So his mask had an LP record for the face, slides for eyes and compact discs for ears. Another wanted to make a statement about the environment and waste. His mask was a found metal object with handles for ears. It was ideal: the only design intervention it required was for two holes to be drilled for eyes.

As the masks developed, so we were able to draw out the essence of the exercise. In particular, we were able to define the links between the ancient art of mask-making and modern graphic communication. Just as a mask will draw attention, alter perception, conceal and then reveal, so graphic design can play the same visual tricks with the way we look at things and understand them.

In particular, the most wonderful African masks capture the spirit and the essence of things without necessarily showing the whole image. A bird mask may suggest a bird by simply making a visual abstraction, with a colour or beak outline perhaps. Graphic design has the same power to summarize and capture the spirit.

Such is the weight of symbolic meaning carried by the mask that its design elements must be carefully and sparingly judged to achieve maximum impact.

This lesson was not lost on the students.

One can argue, of course, that the modern-day role of the mask is all about trickery, seduction and entertainment. And this could be said to go against the concept of Danish design which has traditionally been concerned with honesty and truth to materials.

But at a time when the Danmarks Designskole is expanding its international horizons and raising awareness of the implications of the new Europe-wide markets for design which are opening up, it is somehow appropriate to be examining the guile and sophistication associated with the mask.

Danish design will inevitably undergo change and development in response to the international marketplace.

Danmarks Designskole plans to be in the vanguard of that development, and I was delighted to play a small part in the educational process through the workshop.

Of course we'll go on collecting masks at Pentagram – and now we have a collection of enterprising student masks on slides as a memento of my Danish experience.

KATHERINE McCOY

USA

Countering the tradition
of the apolitical designer

September 1993

T his decade finds us in a crisis of values in the United States. Our increasingly multicultural society is experiencing a breakdown in shared values – national values, tribal values, personal values, even family values – consensual motivating values that create a common sense of purpose in the community.

The question is how can a heterogeneous society develop shared values and yet encourage cultural diversity and personal freedom? Designers and design education are part of the problem, and can be part of the answer. We cannot afford to be passive anymore. Designers must be good citizens and participate in the shaping of our government. As designers we could use our particular talents and skills to encourage others to wake up and participate as well.

Before the US congratulates itself too much on the demise of Communism, we must remember that our American capitalist democracy is not what it used to be either. Much of our stagnation comes from this breakdown of values. Entrepreneurial energy and enthusiastic work ethic have deteriorated into self-interest, complacency, corporate greed, and resentment between ethnic groups and economic classes. Our traditional common American purpose is fading – that sense of building something new where individuals could progress through participating in a system that provided opportunity. Consumerism and materialism now seem to be the only ties that bind. The one group that seems to be bound by more than this is the Far Right; but their bond is regressive, a desire to force fundamentalist prescriptive values on the rest of us.

We have just experienced the Reagan era during which we were told it was all okay, that we could spend and consume with no price tag attached. During this period, graphic designers enjoyed the spoils of artificial prosperity with the same passive hedonism as the rest of the country. Now we are beginning to realize it was not all okay. The earth is being poisoned, its resources depleted, and the US has gone from a creditor to a debtor nation. Our self-absorption and lack of activism has left a void filled by minority single-issue groups aggressively pushing their concerns.

There are serious threats to our civil liberties in the United

States from both fundamentalist censorship of the Right and political correctness from the Left. We have seen the dismemberment of artistic freedom at the National Endowment for the Arts in the past three years and aggressive attempts to censor public schools' teaching from Darwin to Hemingway to safe sex. And as graphic designers specializing in visual communications, the content of our communications may be seriously curtailed if we do not defend our freedom of expression.

But even more troubling is our field's self-censorship. How many graphic designers today would feel a loss if their freedom of expression was handcuffed? Most of our colleagues never exercise their right to communicate on public issues or potentially controversial content. Remove our freedom of speech and graphic designers might never notice. We have trained a profession that feels political or social concerns are either extraneous to our work, or inappropriate.

Thinking back to 1968, the atmosphere at Unimark International during my first year of work typified this problem. Unimark (an idealistic international design office with Massimo Vignelli and Jay Doblin as vice-presidents and Herbert Bayer on the Board) was dedicated to the ideal of the rationally objective professional. The graphic designer was to be the neutral transmitter of the client's messages. Clarity and objectivity were the goal. During that year, the designers I worked with, save one notable exception, were all remarkably uninterested in the social and political upheavals taking place around us. Vietnam was escalating with body counts touted on every evening newscast, the New Left rioted before the Democratic National Convention in Chicago, Martin Luther King and Robert Kennedy were assassinated, and Detroit was still smoking from its riots just down the street from our office. Yet hardly a word was spoken on these subjects. We were encouraged to wear white lab coats, perhaps so that the messy external environment would not contaminate our surgically clean detachment.

These white lab coats make an excellent metaphor for the apolitical designer, cherishing the myth of universal value-free design – that design is a clinical process akin to chemistry, scientifically pure and neutral, conducted in a sterile laboratory environment with precisely predictable results. Yet Lawrence and Oppenheimer and a thousand other examples teach us that even chemists and physicists must have a contextual view of their work in the social/political world around them.

During that time, I became increasingly interested in the social idealism of the times: the civil rights movement, the anti-Vietnam peace movement, the anti-materialism and social experimentation of the New Left, and radical feminism. Yet it was very difficult to relate these new ideas to the design that I was practising and the communication process that I loved so much. Or perhaps the difficulty was not the values of design so much as the values of design community. About all I could connect with was designing and sending (to appalled family members) an anti-Vietnam feminist Christmas card and silk-screening t-shirts with a geometricized "Swiss" version of the feminist symbol. Meanwhile, we continued to serve the corporate and advertising worlds with highly "professional" design solutions.

The implication of the word "professional" as we use it is indicative of the problem here. How often do we hear, "Act like a professional" or "I'm a professional, I can handle it". Being a professional means to put aside one's personal reactions regardless of the situation and to carry on. Prostitutes, practitioners of the so-called oldest profession, must maintain an extreme of cool objectivity about this most intimate of human activities, highly disciplining their personal responses to deliver an impartial and consistent product to their clients.

But passing years and different national contexts have brought different results from the application of these Modernist design paradigms. The myth of objectivity unfortunately does much to disengage the designer from compassionate concerns. Strongly held personal convictions would seem to be inappropriate for the cool-headed objective professional. Functionalism is narrowly defined in measurable utilitarian terms. Too often this means serving the client's definition of function – generally profits – over other concerns, including safety, the environment, and social/cultural/political/environmental impacts. Universalism has brought us the homogenized proper corporate style based mainly on Helvetica and the grid, ignoring the power and potential of regional, idiosyncratic, personal or culturally specific stylistic vocabularies. And the ideal of value-free design is a dangerous myth. In fact all design solutions carry a bias, either explicit or implicit. The more honest designs acknowledge their biases openly rather than manipulate their audiences with assurances of universal "truth" and purity.

Abstraction, Modernism's revolutionary contribution to the visual language of art and design, further distances both designer and audience from involvement. Stripped of imagery, self-referential abstraction is largely devoid of symbols and disconnected from experience in the surrounding world, cool and low on emotion. Abstraction is predictable in application, polite, inoffensive and not too meaningful – thereby providing a safe vocabulary for corporate materials. Imagery, on the other hand, is richly loaded with symbolic encoded meaning, often ambiguous and capable of arousing the entire range of human emotions. Imagery is difficult to control, even dangerous or controversial, often leading to unintended personal interpretations on the part of the audience – but also poetic, powerful and potentially eloquent.

The Modernist agenda has conspired to promote an attitude of apoliticism among American designers, design educators and students, building on the pragmatic American tendency to avoid political dialectics. American designers consistently take European theories and strip them of their political content. Of the various strains of Modernism, many of which were socially concerned or politically revolutionary, American design either chose those most devoid of political content or stripped the theories of their original political idealism.

This ideal of the dispassionate professional distances us from ethical and political values. Think of the words used to describe the disciplined objective professional, whether it be scientist, doctor or lawyer: impartial, dispassionate, disinterested. These become pejorative terms in a difficult world crying for compassion, interest, concern, commitment and involvement. Disinterest is appropriate for a neutral arbitrator but not for an advocate. In fact, most often design education trains students to think of themselves as passive arbitrators of the message between the client/sender and audience/receiver, rather than as advocates for the message content of the audience. Here is the challenge – how to achieve the objectivity and consistency of professionalism without stripping oneself of personal convictions.

Our concept of graphic design professionalism has been largely shaped, and generally for the better, by the legacy of twentieth-century Modernism as it has come to us through the Bauhaus and Swiss lineages. However, there are several dominant aspects of this Modernist ethic that have done much to distance designers from their cultural milieu. The ideals, forms, methods and mythology of Modernism are a large part of this problem of detachment, including the paradigms of universal form, abstraction, self-referentialism, value-free design, rationality and objectivity.

Objective rationalism, particularly that of the Bauhaus, provided a much needed antidote to the sentimentality and gratuitous eclecticism found in nineteenth-century mass production, visual communications and architecture. Linked to functionalism, objective analysis formed the basis of problem-solving methods to generate functional design solutions to improve the quality of daily life. Expanded more recently to include systems design, this attitude has done much to elevate the quality of design thinking.

Linked to the ideal of the objective clear-sighted designer is the ideal of value-free universal forms. Perhaps a reaction to the frequent political upheavals between European nations, especially World War I, early Modern designers hoped to find internationalist design forms and attitudes that would cross those national, ethnic and class barriers that had caused such strife. In addition, a universal design – one design for all – would be appropriate for the classless mass society of industrial workers envisioned by early twentieth-century social reformers.

More recently we have seen a strong interest in French literary theory. But its original element of French contemporary Marxism has been largely ignored in the US, perhaps rightly so. The American political environment is far different from the European; European political dialectics may not be appropriate to us. Yet we cannot assume that no political theory is needed to ground our work – all designers need an appropriate framework to evaluate and assess the impacts of their work within its social/ethical/political milieu. Perhaps this evaluative framework is different for each individual, dependent on the values of each, reflecting our strong tradition of American individualism.

Designers must break out of the obedient, neutral, servant-to-industry mentality, an orientation that was particularly strong in the Reagan/Thatcher 1980s, and continues to dominate design management and strategic design. Yes, we are problem-solvers responding to the needs of the client. But we must be careful of the problems we take on. Should one help sell tobacco and alcohol or design a Presidential memorial library for a man who reads only pulp cowboy novels? Design is not a neutral value-free process. A design has no more integrity than its purpose or subject matter. Garbage in, garbage out. The most rarefied design solution can never surpass the quality of its content.

A dangerous assumption is that corporate work of innocuous content is devoid of political bias. The vast majority of student design projects deal with corporate needs, placing a heavy priority on the corporate economic sector of our society. Commerce is where we are investing our assets of time, budgets, skills and creativity. This is a decisive vote for economics over other potential concerns, including social, educational, cultural, spiritual and political needs. This is a political statement in itself, both in education and practice.

How does one educate graphic design students with an understanding of design as a social and political force? Can a political consciousness be trained? Can an educator teach values? The answer is probably no in the simplistic sense. However, the field of education has a well-developed area referred to as values clarification that offers many possibilities for graphic design educators. Too often we take individuals with eighteen years of experience and strip them of their values, rather than cultivate them for effective application in design practice.

In teaching, these issues must be raised from the beginning for the design student. This is not something to spring on the advanced student after their attitudes have been fixed on neutrality. At the core of this issue is the content of the projects we assign from the very first introductory exercise. Most introductory graphic design courses are based on abstract formal exercises inherited from the Bauhaus and the classic Basle school projects. The detachment problem begins here. These projects either deal with completely abstract form – point, line and plane, for instance – or they remove imagery from context. The graphic translation projects, so effective in training a keen formal sense, unfortunately use a process of abstractional analysis, thereby stripping imagery of its encoding symbolism. (I have to admit to being guilty of this in my assignments in past years.) Divorcing design form from content or context is a lesson in passivity, implying that graphic form is something separate and unrelated to subjective values or even ideas. The first principle is that all graphic projects must have content.

The type of content in each assignment is crucial. It is disheartening to see the vast number of undergraduate projects dedicated to selling goods and services in the marketplace, devoid of any mission beyond business success. Undoubtedly all students need experience in this type of message and purpose. But cannot projects cover a broad mix of content, including issues beyond business? Cultural, social and political subjects make excellent communications challenges for student designers.

Project assignments can require content developed by the student dealing with public and personal, social, political and economic issues and current events. The responsibility for developing content is a crucial one; it counteracts the passive design role in which one unquestioningly accepts client-dictated copy. On a practical level, we know how frequently all designers modify and improve client copywriting; many graphic designers become quite good writers and editors, so closely is our function allied to writing. In a larger sense, however, self-developed content and copy promotes two important attitudes in a design student. One is the ability to develop personal content and subject matter, and an interest in personal design work, executed independently of client assignments. This method of working is much like that of fine artists who find their reward in the self-expression of personal issues. Secondly, the challenge to develop subject matter stimulates the design student to determine what matters on a personal level. A process of values clarification must go on in the student before a subject or subject matter position can be chosen. And the breadth of concerns chosen as subjects by fellow students exposes each student to a wider range of possibilities.

The critique process for issue-oriented work can be a very effective forum for values clarification. This is particularly true of group critiques in which all students are encouraged to participate, rather than the authoritarian traditionalist crit in which the faculty do all the speaking. In evaluating the success or failure of a piece of graphic communications, each critic must address the subject matter and understand the design student's stated intentions before weighing a piece's success. This expands the critique discussion beyond the usual and necessary topics of graphic method, form and technique. Tolerance as well as objectivity are required of each critique participant, in that they must accept and understand the student's intended message before evaluating the piece.

For instance, recently two fundamentalist Christian students brought their religiously-oriented work to our Cranbrook graphic design crits during a two-semester period. It was a challenge – and a lesson in tolerance – for the other students to put aside their personal religious (or non-religious) convictions in order to give these students and their work a fair critique from a level playing field. It was quite remarkable – and refreshing – to find us all discussing spirituality as legitimate subject matter. This has held true for many other subjects from the universe of issues facing our culture today, including local and global environmental issues, animal rights, homelessness, feminism and reproductive choice.

The point here is content. As design educators, we cast projects almost as a scientist designs a laboratory experiment. The formula and the variables conspire to slant the results in one direction or another. The project assignment and the project critique are powerful tools that teach far more than explicit goals, and carry strong implicit messages about design and designers' roles.

Design history also offers a rich resource for understanding the relationship of form and content to socio-political contexts. We all know how often works from art and design history are venerated (and imitated) in an atmosphere divorced from their original context. By exploring the accompanying cultural/social/ political histories, students can see the contextual interdependencies and make analogies to their present time.

Am I advocating the production of a generation of designers preoccupied with political activism, a kind of reborn 1960s' mentality? I think rather what I have in mind is nurturing a crop of active citizens, informed, concerned participants in society who happen to be graphic designers. We must stop inadvertently training our students to ignore their convictions and be passive economic servants. Instead, we must help them to clarify their personal values and to give them the tools to recognize when it is appropriate to act on them. I do think this is possible. We still need objectivity, but this includes the objectivity to know when to invoke personal biases and when to set them aside. Too often our graduates and their work emerge as charming mannequins, voiceless mouthpieces for the messages of ventriloquist clients. Let us instead give designers their voices so they may participate and contribute more fully in the world around them.

JAN RAJLICH

Czech Republic

Comenius and visual education

Icographic, 11, 1977

A short article which concentrates solely on the pictorial aspects of the work of Comenius is no substitute for a detailed study of his entire output. Nor can it offer profound insights into this particular aspect of his work. The aim of my work is much more modest.

It is not to draw your attention to the seventeenth-century Czech thinker's personality, or at least only in general terms.

Some years ago, his work was commemorated by Unesco, which was appropriate, given its role as heir to Comenius' progressive, reforming ideas in education and for the general enlightenment of society. To those far from Comenius' native country, and moreover in a professional journal concerned with visual communication, I should like to mention that Comenius was not only a famous pedagogue and philosopher who, by putting education of the senses to the fore in human education, initiated the real modernization of education - but also belongs among the pioneers who urged an expansion of visual forms of education.

I should also like to remind graphic designers that Comenius discovered the significance of graphic representation as a fundamental means of communication in the effort to convey new knowledge and a new description of the world.

By reprinting the contemporary illustrations to Comenius' writings, I hope to show present-day book and graphic designers the aesthetic charm of this early graphic expression. Such charm is often incidental to the purposes of its authors, so that for the modern observer it has the additional attraction of a certain "unintentional charm".

Both the text and the pictures have a common aim: to remind us of the inspired way in which every artist makes use of the resources available to him. It is desirable that we should follow in the same spirit.

The years 1592 and 1670 mark the beginning and end of the life of Jan Amos Komensky (in Latin, Comenius). These dates are separated by almost eight decades of unrelenting and productive work, not only for Comenius' personal pleasure and pains, but also for his endangered church - the Unity of Czech Brethren - and the

Heaven

well-being of the whole Czech nation. Eight decades, of which Comenius spent less than half in his native country and the rest in exile, were crammed with untiring literary, scientific, cartographic and pedagogical study, along with his work as a preacher. Comenius was a painstaking organizer, not least in the field of politics. He is one of those great polymathic examples from the Renaissance and Baroque periods. His literary and theoretical works, written in Czech and Latin, are so extensive that the recent critical edition published in Czechoslovakia consists of about forty-five volumes. Yet a substantial part of his treatise, *Pansophiae*, together with other manuscripts, was burnt in a fire in one of his temporary retreats.

Today, despite the barrier of three centuries, the heritage of Comenius is alive and close to us, the people of the twentieth century. According to Comenius, education and culture are man's essential guide to understanding the complexities of life in this world. We cannot be indifferent to his notion that man's education continues throughout his life. How did he develop this idea? In his *Common Deliberation*, Comenius divides life into separate stages convenient for education and forming a coherent system; at each stage, throughout his life, a man should learn something new. It should be emphasized that Comenius conceives of these individual stages as interlinked; each one conditions the next, and nothing from the previous stage is allowed to lie fallow.

Man possesses all the necessary tools for him to develop through education and take the position in the world appropriate to him. These tools - "intellect, tongue, senses and heart" - are refined by education. The senses enable man to understand nature in an inductive way, while the intellect provides for an understanding of fundamental principles.

Since sharpness of the senses is a precondition of successful intellectual development, Comenius begins his educational system by educating the senses in general, and with visual education in particular. According to his concept, moral education is also based on education of the senses, which forms the reliable basis for further maturing and development of the human personality.

In the second half of the twentieth century, we are looking for new ways of speaking, new ways of describing objects, new forms of communication to cope with the constantly changing play of symbols which represents our experiments in aligning the world with a new chain of events, not only psychological but also in terms of new thoughts about the universe beyond man. Where does the visual artist find his place amongst all this?

Although the search seems highly topical, it is far from being new in European history. We encounter it in the new philosophy related to direct observation of the world, in the philosophy of Francis Bacon - and in works by Comenius. His book entitled *Orbis Sensualium Pictus* (The World in Pictures as Perceived by the

Senses) first appeared in Nuremburg in 1658, from the printer
M. Endter. The aim of the book, in conformity with the author's
theory that man must be directly acquainted with things (see *Didactica Magna*), was to represent a series of objects as perceived by human
senses, each of them depicted and described. God, nature, the
elements, materials, objects, animals, plants, man and his work - man,
the maker of material goods and mental values.

Instead of presenting a single world view, Comenius, by
acquainting his readers with objects, moves towards an understanding
of the world in all its variety of forms as well as its universality. His
descriptions start in a vivid manner by describing how we learn to
speak and the way speech is connected to other concrete sounds.
He gives a notion of the unity of visual perception of things and
their universal significance. In *Orbis Pictus*, woodcuts were the
mediators of comprehension, as Comenius frequently says that sight
is the most important of all the senses.

Orbis Pictus became one of the most popular picture books almost
as soon as it appeared and attracted the attention of his contemporaries
all over Europe. Many further editions were printed, not only in
Nuremburg but also in London, Copenhagen and other cultural
centres of the time.

The book was a great breakthrough in educational practice at a
time when teaching was still primarily oral. Even though illustrated
textbooks had appeared from time to time before Comenius'
period, *Orbis Pictus* was the first one to make the pictures integral
to the text. For whole decades right up to the nineteenth century,
Orbis Pictus was the fundamental textbook of Europe. Many giants
of world culture, from Goethe to Lermontov, were brought up on
this book and it appeared in almost all the European languages.
The foreword to a new edition issued in Brno in 1929 tells us that
there were even Persian and Japanese editions.

Jan Amos Komensky is known to the general public primarily
as an educational reformer. His books were a prime part of this
pioneering work. His *Opera Didactica Omnia* (Collected Didactic
Works, Amsterdam, 1658) outlined daring reforms which,
incidentally, have still not been realized in many countries today.
He wanted uniforms and compulsory education for all children,
with no privileges pertaining to social class, property, race or sex.

Education, he believed, should be based on a well thought-out
method; the syllabus and the organization of schools should be
natural and spontaneous. Classes should cultivate the development
of the senses and of reason, and they should be based on a
knowledge of objects - so teaching aids such as pictures, models
and diagrams play a fundamental role in Comenius' system. The
education system should proceed from fundamental and simple
notions to higher and more complicated ones, from the well-
known to the unknown, from the concrete to the abstract.

Celestial sphere

Because of his constant concern with education, Comenius wrote many textbooks, the most important being in the field of philology, and developed in them the theories he had previously formulated. Through these volumes Comenius achieved lasting success and international fame. His reputation was made immediately on the publication of his Latin textbook *Janua Linguarum Reserata* (The Open Door to Language), in 1631.

This textbook has been republished, rewritten and revised several times, and translated into most European languages. In it, Comenius proceeded from the principle that a language textbook, if it is to be really useful, must not only teach individual words, terse sentences and grammatical rules, but also describe things, and must inform the student about the real world in which he lives. This is the crux of the success of this extraordinary textbook.

In keeping with this principle, Comenius carefully considered the selection of words and grouped them by subject in separate chapters. This was ordered in a sequence so that the book, alongside its lessons in language, showed how the world was created, described living and inanimate nature, especially man, his body and his mental life, his different occupations, and manifestations of social and cultural life such as schools, art, morality and religion.

Its success was only surpassed by that of the *Orbis Pictus*, which is composed along similar lines. Besides his principle of objectively conveying information, Comenius also used his other educational principles of spontaneity, simplicity and making learning fun. He made every effort not only to make the teaching process easier, but also to make learning positively attractive to students through his methods and textbooks.

He reckoned, correctly, that one thing conditions the other.

Position of planets

DEBORAH SUSSMAN

USA

How I got my first job

Graphic design career guide, ed. James Craig,
New York, Watson Guptill, 1992

Before starting my own firm I only had two real jobs – and one was much more than "a job". It affected the course of my life and work forever.

In the early 1950s, the office of Charles and Ray Eames had only fourteen people. Yet it was the most important and exciting design office in the world. When Charles came to lecture at the Institute of Design in Chicago, where I was a third-year student, I felt an immediate affinity – and a premonition. Then, as now, I was a workaholic and could never separate work from play or art from life. I produced a lot. I also could draw, and was fascinated by all the new tools and multi-disciplinary activities at the I.D. I took advantage of the art, acting, and linguistic background inherited from my parents, and learned at Midwood High School in Brooklyn and two years at Bard College. (My plan had been to be an artist as well as an actress. Somehow, to me, the practice of design encompasses both.)

All this plus my optimistic personality prompted the school to recommend me to Charles Eames in response to his request for "someone to come and help with graphics for the summer". But it was really Charles and Ray's friend, the visionary engineer/ architect Konrad Wachsmann, whose recommendation counted the most.

My dedication and obvious care for my work were factors in the school's recommendation. But Konrad really knew what kind of person would "fit" into the intense yet informal, rigorous yet playful, way of life the Eameses maintained. Chemistry has a lot to do with successful professional relationships (even in a giant corporation, where there is one leader with whom you can connect, and the "impossible" can be achieved).

Leaving all my "stuff" behind, I flew to Los Angeles as quickly as possible. I got $2.00 an hour, learned to drive, and never went back to school. Working with Charles and Ray on toys, ads, exhibits, films and showrooms was the best education anyone could ask for. Four years later, I went to Europe with a Fulbright grant, worked for a while in Milan, and got my second real job designing graphics for Galeries Lafayette in Paris.

upholstered lounge chair

Herman Millwer, Eames chair
advertisement

97

Unbelievably to the Eameses and myself – yet to our mutual delight – I worked there again during the 1960s, after three years in Europe. It was only when my "wings" got really noticeable that I left to start on my own. But the connection with Charles and Ray never ended. The way I see the world and the large and complex environmental projects we design at my own office are a result of those glorious years that I was privileged to share.

CHAPTER 3

The Social Role of the Designer

Ruedi Baur
Pierre Bernard
Michael Bierut
Karl Oskar Blase
Pieter Brattinga
Pieter Brattinga
Mimmo Castellano
Ken Cato
Gert Dumbar
Franco Grignani
Herbert W. Kapitzki
Laurence Madrelle
Enzo Mari
Fernando Medina
Kazumaza Nagai
Gérard Paris-Clavel
Michael Peters
Tullio Pericoli
Josep Pla-Narbona
Paula Scher
Niklaus Troxler

RUEDI BAUR

France

Design by subtraction

Lecture: Ecole National des Beaux-Arts, Lyon

S ubtract signs, subtract gadgets, subtract the pointless, subtract the too-much-to-the point, subtract systemisation, subtract formulas, subtract power, subtract signatures, subtract "Oeuvres", subtract security, subtract beliefs, subtract morals, subtract religion, subtract seriousness, subtract décor, subtract the sham, subtract repetition, subtract noise, subtract rambos, subtract ponderousness, subtract sadness, subtract promises, subtract easy facility, subtract the ersatz, subtract opportunism, subtract irresponsibility, subtract snobbishness, subtract compromises, subtract bad compromises, subtract weak excuses, subtract authoritarianism, subtract bits of rubbish, subtract liberalism, subtract inequalities, subtract self-satisfaction, subtract realism, subtract standardisation, subtract conventions, subtract ceremonial, subtract pretence, subtract habits, subtract fears, subtract jealousies, subtract nonsense, subtract nonsenses, subtract bullshit, subtract consultations, subtract copies, subtract models, subtract aestheticism, subtract superficiality, subtract tittle-tattle, subtract sectarianism, subtract corporatism, subtract nationalism, subtract national egotism, subtract certitudes, subtract tin gods, maybe even subtract subtraction?

The idea of "design by subtraction" came into being following a visit to a major exhibition devoted to the design of the 1980s. Together with Enzo Mari, we were discussing how hard it was to find any quality in the profusion of objects claiming "design" styling or aesthetics created in the previous decade. The multiplicity of these shapes – certainly attractive and sometimes novel but too often superficial, linked to "design" more by form and sign than by content – had reduced all the objects produced in recent years to a conglomeration of images ready for indiscriminate consumption or at least for a consumption governed more by fashion than need.

Having made this realization about "design" in today's context of media superficiality, we were led to look around for an alternative to the current formalist quest; not an alternative that would reject the beautiful or return to rationalist theories, but one that would redefine the job of the designer.

Is it not time that our work as designers was cut loose from

100

Plus reduced to minus

purely material ends, was freed from the overproduction of objects, and was allowed to take note again of the other things happening in our society? Is there not a need to bring back into our profession some social aspiration by not restricting ourselves to the interests of the user/consumer but recovering the humanist concept of utility? It is also up to the creator to provide a sense of purpose, not simply by offering the excuse of complying with the instructions he is given in the best possible way but by thinking more about what he is doing, by attempting to see his work as part of a more all-embracing concern and, particularly, by taking account of all the consequences, direct or indirect, short-term or long-term, of what he is currently creating.

Design by subtraction aims to be one of the points of departure for thinking of this kind. Is not creating by doing away with what already exists in itself an act of design? Subtracting a group of houses from an urban environment to create a square or a garden is the most obvious illustration, but how would it work in the field of design? Does not each of our creations begin with an act of subtraction? Where can subtractions be made, what is the purpose of them...?

PIERRE BERNARD

France

The social role of
the graphic designer

Lecture: "The Core of Understanding", Minneapolis, 1991

A rtists have for a long time been heading for ghettos, whether rich or poor. Other people have been subjected to a major mass-media aesthetic – or for the most underprivileged – to its leftovers.

Our Western society is working at two different speeds. For the minority, a world of calm has come into being in which design means authentic quality. Art can be part of every life. It is a world in which a materialised and human reality can develop.

For the rest – the majority – what is offered is exactly the opposite. Art is something to be visited in reservations, and spiritual harmony is to be found in other realms, religious or chemical.

Inequality is on the increase. The humanist dream of a unification of our planet's history in the capitalist logic of multinationals has in practice become a reductive standardization. It has thus been deemed legitimate to give arts and artists the function of entertainment and decoration, while techniques and technicians take care of efficient production.

This division of labour amounts to a complete capitulation as regards the principles on which design is founded. The division between the artist as creator and the artisan as technician has been born again out of the ashes of those founding principles. It marks a return to the Stone Age.

I believe that the single identity of the artist and the technician in the person of the graphic designer forms the basis for his capacity to assert his role strongly – and to take his own specific action as an individual who is a part of civilization. I believe that the social function of the graphic designer is a subject to be approached through opinions and persuasion rather than through logic and knowledge.

"Life will always be hard enough to prevent men from losing the desire for something better," Maxim Gorky said. The graphic designer's social responsibility is based on the wish to take part in the creation of a better world. It seems simple to declare such a principle, but given the contradictions of real life, the principle does not lead readily to practical rules of behaviour.

PIERRE BERNARD

New international order:
"You can't change the world
from the top", illustration
published in *Révolution,* Atelier
de Création Graphique, 1992

A social critique

Any assessment of the social dimension of graphic design must
always be made in a specific concrete situation, and this is a most
difficult task. We all live in society, but not in the same one.
At least, thank God, not yet.

Today, the production of visual communications consists
essentially of advertising. Visual productions in advertising are
hugely sophisticated and articulated in relation to gigantic mass-
media networks. They transcend frontiers and cultural divides.
Their basic critique has been developed by the Marxist critic
John Berger in *Ways of Seeing.* He demonstrates that "glamour"
is a modern invention in terms of images. It is the expression of
the pursuit of individual happiness, considered as a universal right.

Berger goes on to say that "publicity turns consumption into a
substitute for democracy. The choice of what one eats (or wears or
drives) takes the place of significant political choice. Publicity helps
to mask and compensate for all that is undemocratic within society.
And it also masks what is happening in the rest of the world."

There is a difference between advertising and graphic design.
Advertising is today more and more centralized, international,
generalized and, therefore, standardized – like the economic forces
that produce it, and the products it deals with. Graphic design,
on the other hand, continues to be created and to structure itself
in an autonomous and diversified manner – in direct contact with
the specific social fabrics of different societies around the world.
It is this diversity that provides the possibility for the development
of graphic communication across the world in the future.

If we look at simplified representation of graphic communication,
we see that it has transmitting subjects (clients and graphic designers),
messages and objects (goals, ends, products), and receivers
(audiences and consumers) with their needs and expectations.
Second, communication happens in a concrete time frame. The
link between these two propositions gives us the social dimension
of graphic design.

From the point of view of time, one can classify communication
on a scale. At one end of the scale, we find the graphic design that
I call the graphic design of permanence, aiming at the medium
and long term. At the other end of the scale there is an ephemeral
graphic design, aiming at the short term.

From the point of view of space, I also distinguish two major
classes of graphic design: graphic design integrated with either a
physical structure or an identity; and independent graphic design.
We notice that independent graphic design is often short-lived,
whereas integrated graphic design is more permanent, both varying
according to time and place.

103

Permanent graphic design

What is the typical landscape of permanent graphic design?
It consists of architecture and urban design; newspaper grids;
charts, maps and diagrams; reference books such as atlases and
catalogues; calendars, notices, instruction forms and signs; plans
and pictographic systems. They all work toward the visual
expression of a general structural development.

The goal of this kind of graphic design (permanent, integrated)
is achieved by integrating the message (form, content) with society.
It confirms established values and asks that they be accepted.
It transforms the idea, the judgement, and the aesthetic value into
tangible "natural" reality. Generally, graphic design is presented
as functional, but the symbolic role it plays quickly becomes
permanent and takes on a new functionality: ideological integration.

In the recent past, permanent, integrated graphic design
was a vehicle for many humanist aspirations and major progressive
values. Today, in conjunction with the demolition of the mass
media and the gradual shrinking of the world, the goal of social
consensus often leads such design to forget specific social realities
in favour of a higher international model, one that directly produces
packaging. Permanent, integrated graphic design is one of the main
areas of intervention for graphic designers who are conscious of
their social role.

Short-lived graphic design

What is the typical landscape of short-lived graphic design?
Here, in contrast to permanent graphic design, the landscape seems
to include diverse and specific acts: narrations and contradictory,
divergent or opposite affirmations on posters, newspapers,
advertisements, windows, leaflets, programmes, books, exhibitions,
films, videos and so on.

This type of graphic design (ephemeral, independent) aims
at transmitting specific messages linked to specific situations.
Ephemeral, independent graphic design seems to have an operational
nature opposite to the functional nature of integrated, permanent
graphic design. Its products are ephemeral. They attract attention
and then disappear.

Design Renaissance, poster
for the Icograda conference
in Glasgow, Atelier de Création
Graphique, 1993

If this classification – permanent versus ephemeral and integrated
versus independent – is valid, we can conclude that the ideological
consensus is linked to socio-graphic stability. That is, people will
tend to think alike if the visual landscape is structured and unchanging.
And the feeling of freedom is linked to the presence of numerous
and varied disagreements in live exchanges. However, as Berger
has shown us, this "display" of freedom is mere illusion, when the
general strategy behind it leads exclusively to consumption. For
how long, and to what socially progressive ends, comes the feeling
of freedom through consumption?

104

It is this dead-end situation that has led many high-level graphic designers to abandon ephemeral, independent design for the permanent, integrated projects considered to be more worthy.

Designer and client as co-authors

Let us move from the time frame of graphic design and examine the different participants and their relationships.

In the process of communication, the graphic designer and the client together constitute the transmitter. The message will be the result of their collaboration. Who chooses whom? By nature, the client needs the graphic designer only occasionally, whether the arrangement is repetitive or continuous.

Unlike the graphic designer, who looks for a kind of communication that is in relation to the nature of the message and of the presumed receiver, the client's concerns and existence are elsewhere, outside of the communication process. The client looks for what would appear to be a solution (a graphic product) to his problems, in a competitive context. It is for this reason that the client tends to consider communication as strictly instrumental, and the graphic designer as a neutral transmitter of his message. The instrumental conception of visual communication is often the one adopted by clients who themselves have a very narrow view of their own role as transmitter.

But can neutral aesthetics exist? Can the message of the client always be unequivocal, never ambiguous? The truth between the client and the graphic designer will always be a complex and subjective truth. Otherwise, this collaboration has no reason to exist and can be advantageously replaced by a mechanical act.

It is through the contact established at the outset of the collaboration with the designer that the client can be brought to widen his perspective and transform his desire in order to obtain, among other things, that result. It is this contact that can make him conscious of his cultural role and his power of decision over the time frame of the communication.

The designer would like to choose a client for his apparent social role. The client — whose pragmatism about cost influences his demands — chooses the designer because of his know-how in relation to the economics of production. The depth of the relationship depends to a considerable extent on the nature of the consideration the client has for the know-how of graphic design. While many small-scale clients in the social, cultural, political, and even economic fields have high expectations of graphic designers, many others with considerable social influence are unaware of graphic design or have a very simplistic conception of it.

It will be absolutely essential, in the years ahead, to make graphic design known in its complete technical, intellectual, and artistic dimension. Then, graphic designers will be in a position to identify and respond consciously to requests that generate social acts that they can support in their role as co-authors.

This notion of co-authorship seems essential to me, from an ethical point of view. The necessary co-operation between client and graphic designer will lead the client to share the aesthetic position (not devoid of ideology) of the designer, and it will lead the designer to accept the validity of the ideological position of his client. It is this particular balance between co-authors that allows the production to be oriented toward a cultural act, which, by definition, is always risky.

If this important notion does not operate in the client-graphic designer relationship, then it becomes a service relationship only. And under these conditions, professional responsibility becomes a delusion.

The graphic designer and the receiver

The relationship between the graphic designer and the receiver can work efficiently only in the presence of the client. The notion of quality shared by the client and the designer will be determined by the respect in which the receiver is held. This appreciation will be expressed in the cultural level of the message (form, content) in relation to the present cultural level of the receiver.

If social and cultural measuring devices can be used to give valuable information about receivers, they can also be used to consider the receivers simply as military "targets", where the objective has to be achieved by any means. Such measurement can also lead to a communications strategy based on the isolation of the general public into typecast groups. By crystallizing diversity, it transforms a group of free-ranging citizens into several small groups of specialized consumers.

One of the major social functions of graphic design is quite the opposite: broadening the cultural horizon of the public directly concerned.

DEMAIN SE DECIDE AUJOURD HUI
"Tomorrow is decided upon today", Atelier de Création Graphique, 1992

The relationship between the graphic designer and the receiver also works within the mediation of the message. In most cases, this mediation imposes a one-way communication. The communication does not communicate: it soliloquizes. The right to respond on equal terms does not exist.

The situation forces the two subjects of the communication, client and graphic designer, into social isolation. The client's status is one of power, and his isolation in mediated communication leads him to want more power. The social status of the graphic designer is one of dependence. Confronted with his isolation, there are two directions he can take: one toward greater dependence on the client; the other toward a greater awareness of the balance needed in the communication process. The less specialized they are in a repetitive relationship with the client, the more freedom the designer will have to make the choice to become the receiver's silent ally.

The graphic designer and the message

It is through the message that the graphic designer as co-author finally confronts his or her knowledge, culture, conceptions and sincerity. The graphic designer must define a strategy and be aware of other existing social strategies, including those that arise from different national situations. In relation to the message, the graphic designer applies pertinent expression codes – whether derived from local, national, or international culture – thus producing emotion and meaning. As in Baudelaire's *Les Fleurs du mal,* this capacity of graphic designers to find paths through the "dark forest of signs" makes them artists in the full sense.

If one conceives one's work as being based on the status of a technician and an artist, this implies having a general cultural objective that goes beyond merely giving form to an operational discourse.

This "going beyond" tells us we cannot be satisfied with the practice of ephemeral graphic design that has no relation to (or is in disagreement with) a global society. Nor can professional satisfaction arise from a permanent graphic design that remains unaltered despite the struggles and historical changes of the world it purports to reflect.

For this reason, it becomes necessary to link ephemeral and permanent, integrated and independent, in order to assert an articulate, complex cultural conception that is not élitist, populist or reductive. Therefore, social graphic design corresponds to the cultural dimension of the message, to its articulation in a long-term project of cultural development, where the permanent-integrated (strategy) and the ephemeral-independent (tactic) are not in contradiction.

In opposition to the standardized profusion of advertising, we must work from particular social situations – from their specific dynamics and their manageable human dimensions. It is from these that small communications units will be able to build creative works that will regenerate and develop the visual riches already attained by society.

If the moral values that founded graphic design have almost disappeared in favour of those of triumphant marketing, they continue to underlie the awareness of many designers and students scattered around the world. It is this consciousness that must be encouraged and maintained. We can hope to see these values flourish openly within the different social realities to come.

MICHAEL BIERUT

USA

The Thrill is Gone (Almost)

AIGA, Chicago, Spring 1980

Design is, in the end, made by designers. Over the past decade, without anyone noticing, this fact has become increasingly inconvenient. More and more, what is made has become detached from the people who make it.

Most of us don't become graphic designers intending to change the world or to make piles of money; there are too many easier ways to do either. Instead, we become designers because at some point in our lives we draw a picture, or combine words and images, or visualize an idea, and experience what might be called the thrill of creation. A moment ago, something didn't exist; now it does, and I made it happen.

Of course, sooner or later we learn to use this thrill for other purposes – to change the world, to make money – but, for most of us, the excitement of creation came first. This motivation proceeds from a very direct, passionate connection between a designer and his or her work.

For many of us, this connection is forged early on in design school. The problems are relatively open-ended with few "real-world" limitations; the instructors may challenge us, but ultimately nurture our responses; and the best solutions come from the heart: essentially, good design in design school pleases no one but its maker.

Coming to grips with the "real world"

Then comes the real world, and challenge after challenge to this bond between the designer and the work. Not only do the assignments suddenly come with budgets and deadlines attached, but in place of supportive teachers, the young designer is confronted with employers who change the work, clients who reject it, focus groups who don't understand it, and audiences who often just don't care.

In the face of all this, we have only that fragile thrill, a barely formed sense of confidence in our judgments, and the passion that drove us into the field to begin with. After two or three years, a lot of designers learn that what they thought would be a crusade is, in fact, just a job.

And designers, like anyone else, find that their priorities change as they mature. Starting out, we view our counterparts in the worlds of finance and commerce with faint contempt, interviewing for their jobs at investment banks and market research firms with nothing to show but shined shoes and firm handshakes. How lucky to be a designer, where our qualifications are right there in our portfolios, and we can pick our noses during the interview if our work's good enough! How wonderful to actually make something for a living and not just move numbers and kiss butt all day!

Unfortunately, ten years on, we start to encounter clients our own age, and sooner or later, we learn that one of them is one of those pitiable bankers who just happens to have gotten a bonus more than triple our annual salary. And the obvious rejoinder – "Yeah, but did you get anything in the *Print Regional Annual?*" – sounds more lame than crushing. That special compensation, the connection to your work, can seem more and more trivial and immature.

These challenges have always existed in our field, yet the best designers have always managed to keep passion alive. Those who failed to do so, who compromised their vision, who sold out for financial gain or mere expediency, who simply got burnt out, risk being labelled as hacks.

At least they used to. For, it seems to me, the 1980s have at last created a middle ground, an alternative to hackdom. Its name is professionalism.

The hidden cost of professionalism
In the last decade, the vision of a designer as a person with unique, uncompromised vision has given way to the designer as team player, component in the marketing mix, and self-effacing advancer of long- and short-term corporate goals. In place of the messy ordeal of maintaining a passionate connection with one's work, we are offered whatever satisfaction that exists in pleasing others who determine the criteria for success and failure. Design, once a means of expression, has become a commodity in an ever-expanding marketplace.

It is this point of view that has made possible the assembly of giant, "global" design firms, as well as the acquisition of smaller groups by larger ones. Implicit in each buyout agreement is that the designers of the acquired firm are important but ultimately expendable, and that the equity of the firm resides not in mercurial human beings but in some more abstract notion of "reputation" or "philosophy".

Global design organizations are necessarily based on the premise that "good" designers are interchangeable, and that institutional will is ultimately more potent than individual passion. Nonetheless, design isn't made by philosophies or organizational charts. Design, same as ever, is made by designers.

In the coming decade, we may find ourselves looking back

wistfully to a time when giants trod the earth. The heroes of
our profession – designers as diverse as Paul Rand, Milton Glaser,
Ivan Chermayeff, Massimo Vignelli and Seymour Chwast – are
unmistakably a dying breed. Typified by a single-minded devotion
to their work and an unwillingness to substitute marketable
competence for a riskier brand of brilliance, they seem more and
more anachronistic in today's environment.

Most of us could name younger designers who seem motivated
by a similar sense of mission. However, while the number of
practising designers increases each year at a rate that could be called
epidemic, the heirs to Rand and Glaser seem fewer and farther
between. And increasingly, their work is limited to the fringes of
the business, to those few clients who will always be eager to take
risks. These designers have been driven to the periphery not by
hacks but by professionals.

Upholders of "professionalism" would argue – quite reasonably
– that design exists to serve the client first, not to satisfy the
creative needs of the designer. But would anyone doubt that IBM
was well-served by Paul Rand? And would anyone suggest that
Rand failed to satisfy himself first?

No one would argue that "professionalism" and all it implies
is in itself bad for graphic design. Certainly we all crave more
credibility for our field in the business community. Certainly we
want to be indispensable to our clients, and certainly design is,
among other things, a business.

Nonetheless, what brought so many of us to graphic design
in the beginning was a single, momentary thrill of creation. Today
there are many pressures to betray this primal impulse and invent
a substitute for passionate dedication to the work itself. There is no
substitute. I am convinced that, above anything else, sustaining this
connection is what creates great work and great, not competent,
not professional, but great designers, and is where the hope of our
field – our profession – will lie in the 1990s.

KARL OSKAR BLASE

Germany

...terribly utopian

Texte über Kunst und Visuelle Kommunikation,
Munich, Verlag Silke Schreiber, 1991

The fact that today exhibitions of commercial art are part of the programme at museums and galleries is a sign that it is regarded as part of our cultural life. And this is not just because it has a close link with art and as a kind of "applied art" is a companion to "free art", but also because we know that it can create a connection between the requirements of everyday life and the artistic areas of our life. It is particularly interesting that through such an exhibition the dual significance of poster art becomes clearer.

However, it also becomes clearer that the culturally enhanced "concern" which can be detected in the atmosphere of a gallery corresponds very little to the outside art world. Since whatever is highlighted in exhibitions is always just a fraction of what reaches us through advertising columns, magazines and in shop windows. And if we consider how the mass of advertising fulfils its mercantile purpose without any artistic reference and ambitions, we recognize the ambiguity of our work as graphic designers in an "intellectually cultural" world on the one hand and in a commercial, pragmatic world on the other hand. The "unity of art and life" is an expression reserved for speeches. In our era of rational thinking, it seems impossible to make this unity a reality. We, as poster designers, don't want to set ourselves up as moralists either when we maintain that art exists exclusively, virtually without any influence on our surroundings, and commercial art rarely exists in natural harmony with our vital living conditions and social demands.

In this connection an event is of interest which took place in the summer of 1962 in New York. An event which made the vacuum which exists between our surroundings and our art world visible. In New York a new artistic direction was born overnight: Pop Art. A kind of advertising already belonged to popular culture which is spread throughout the whole world and which includes the many Coca-Cola girls, the super car radiator, comic strips etc. Pop culture can be translated as popular culture but also as culture which goes off with a bang. There was quite a stir in the New York art world when a few young and previously unknown artists, who for the most part were trained as commercial artists, declared pop culture to be art. They exhibited pictures painted in the style

111

of comic strips, soft drinks posters and magazine advertisements. Everything conceivable which is available to us each and every day was on show in huge oil paintings in the renowned galleries of New York. Strawberry and vanilla ice cream, ties, car radiators, roast chickens, fur coats, sardines and painted fingernails. Everything painted in the style of banal advertisements. Roy Lichtenstein, one of these Pop Artists, had an exhibition in the avant-garde Galerie Castelli and sold all his paintings. It was a huge success, although the New York art scene pulled these angry young men apart. Thomas Messer from the Guggenheim Museum declared in a lecture that these artists were influenced by Léger and the Museum of Modern Art bought a "Rote Strumpfhose auf hellblauen Grund" by Claes Oldenburg.

The same thing happened at the Stedelijk Museum in Amsterdam. Martial Raysse bought countless items made from plastic and put together the following in one room: plastic balls, plastic gloves, plastic umbrellas, all kinds of plastic animals, people made from plastic, life jackets, a musical box, a radio, string shopping bags, bottles, buckets, cups, sunglasses, a swimming pool, a neon sign.

Martial Raysse and the Pop Artists are pushing forward even more persistently than their predecessors, the Neo-Dadaists, such as Tinguely, who welded together old sewing machines, motorbikes and other items from scrapyards to make a non-utility machine – i.e. also familiar objects but this time things that have essentially disappeared from view and are only brought back to the present through the will of the artist.

The Pop Artists, on the other hand, turn to the things we see around us at the moment and elevate them to art. What is interesting for us here is purely the fact that these young artists take their subjects from the world of advertising and we recognize that what is portrayed is a representation of our fully painted surroundings; the fact that it is framed and exhibited here shocks us, though we take it for granted outside the confines of the ceremonious gallery, ultimately accepting it as our cultural environment.

The importance of these events as art should not be over-emphasized here, yet this is certainly more than just a case of having fun. And it shouldn't be said that any common ground exists between the intentions of the Pop Artists and the Novum group.

Exhibition installation, 1956

Novum is actually going about things the other way round and is trying to bring art into our everyday lives, to create a link between purpose and form, and in this we see the special qualities of commercial art if it can be extended beyond its trite traditional application. On the other hand pop culture is what we have been trying to overcome for five decades and in retrospect we can say that modern commercial art is no longer in its infancy and we can feel that we have come through the "advertising era". In particular, the basic ideas which originated in the 1920s haven't lost their power

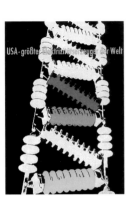

Poster, Karl Oskar Blase, 1954

of communication today – Bauhaus and De Stijl, for example.

Having overcome the unrestrained advertising style, Lucian Bernhard proved back in 1915 with his Manoli poster that even a factual poster can be promotional and artistic without the need for literary details. Whilst later on, around 1925, designers such as Herbert Bayer, Jan Tschichold, Anton Stankowsky, Piet Zwart and Hans Leistikow using modern elements from photography and typography provided a contemporary, independent commercial art form.

A piece of commercial art which is connected with the development of industry cannot submit to it unconditionally. Admittedly it helps that what is produced is also sold and used. The cycle from "producing to consuming" is vital today and actually there's nothing awful about it. Graphic designers, however, have a significant responsibility for the fact that our economic goods which are produced and consumed so fast also become cultural goods boosted by their recommendations. This means giving honest information about honest products, since if you total up all the publications which reach all of us over a period of time, they can determine the social and aesthetic conduct of whole generations.

Therefore in our opinion, commercial art today has the task of being a component of art above and beyond its mercantile purpose, which connects industry and culture. Perhaps even, and this is of course very utopian, our art world will become an integral part of our own environment.

The question of the direction taken by art is consequently of secondary importance. And this exhibition isn't about creating a new style, but more about many kinds of commercial art and poster art finding their own individual form of expression. Since art which is otherwise linked to a particular purpose is free here, it may even be more liberated than "free art", which has its own market principles, which are often not determined by the artist to the extent they may seem to be.

PIETER BRATTINGA

Netherlands

Design in a finite world

The planning of future production, 1976

n our consumer society, over the last forty years, we have come to accept that a great variety of necessary and unnecessary products will be available all the time. This has led to overproduction and competition, which in turn has led to the virtual exhaustion of all kinds of resources.

If people could be taught that by reducing their daily consumption their health would benefit and the life-span of their children and grandchildren would increase, planners could begin a new system of world production.

Once people had accepted the idea of eating simply and buying fewer or no unnecessary products, the producers and leaders of industry could introduce a new production strategy. It would be based on using fewer materials, materials that could be recycled, and on making products last longer.

At the same time, industrial leaders would create teams of designers, sociologists, distribution experts and others to plan the most economical forms of production, marketing and distribution. Design can only play an important role if it is part of an overall economic plan which is geared to saving energy in every possible way.

PIETER BRATTINGA

Netherlands

Public and private:
Dutch design, 1945-91

Print, New York, November/December 1991

Thbe Netherlands is a small country with some fifteen million inhabitants, situated on the western border of Germany and north of France and Belgium. A large part of the Netherlands is bordered by the North Sea, with England on the opposite shore. Surrounded by German, French and English speaking countries, the Netherlands feels the influence of its neighbours and of their language and semantics on a daily basis in its trade and shipping.

Once an aggressive country, the Netherlands showed its strength by conquering faraway places as if it were a big power. Its position as a center of trade and shipping brought influences from many other nations to the Dutch people. One could say, too, that Amsterdam – as the last port of call before the voyage to a new land – became a "free town" for many passing through who wished to settle in other countries. This flow of nationalities through the Netherlands created an atmosphere of tolerance for different cultures and languages, and an openness to new ideas of all kinds.

During the early part of this century, many people in the southern part of the Netherlands still spoke French and the wealthy often sent their children to French-speaking schools. Later, before World War II, there was a tendency to pay more attention to the German language and literature and to the politics of the new Germany under Hitler. The war, however, changed this admiration for the new order to a hatred of the German occupation forces, who compelled schoolchildren to give up French in favour of the study of German, which was obligatory in elementary schools. During the war, but especially toward its end, Dutch children secretly started learning English as some of their parents listened, also secretly, to the BBC. Thus one can see that the influence of other languages changed dramatically during a timespan of only about fifty years. After the war ended in 1945, English became more and more popular not only because of the presence of the Allied armies, but also because of the influence of radio, and more recently, television with all its English and American programs. Clearly, the Dutch have always been influenced by international communication.

115

The poverty of the Netherlands in 1945 was not as severe as the poverty in Germany, but food, raw materials and services were scarce. Food was still rationed, as were leather for shoes and paper for printing. While neighbouring Belgium was quite well off because of its rich colony, the Belgian Congo, which had supplied bauxite for the manufacture of aeroplanes, the Dutch were not so fortunate: far from supplying wealth, their colony, the Netherlands East Indies, was fighting a war of independence. The Dutch in their poverty looked with envy to Belgium where one could buy such luxuries as nylon stockings and oranges, and where one saw huge six-sheet posters from the US urging support for American industry, which had already invested in Belgium. Slowly, with the help of the Marshall Plan, the Netherlands began building its own textile and shoe industries, and, with an effort that many had considered impossible, was able to take its place among the industrialized nations of Europe.

In this time of poverty and paper rationing, Dutch designers developed ingenious solutions to the paper shortages by creating posters on which a few basic colors were overprinted to produce many other colors. Among those who were masters in this field were Otto Treumann, Dick Elffers and Jan Bons. During the war, designers like Treumann had worked for the Resistance by copying identity papers and even bank notes. They also refused to join the German *Kultur Kammer*, the authorized register of recognized artists, thereby eliminating the possibility of any official commission. And they dreamed of a new beginning after the war was over.

Willem Sandberg, a typographic designer who was curator of the Stedelijk Museum in Amsterdam before the war and became its director afterwards, wrote in 1955 about that period: "War is hard. It provides a period of reflection in which we can separate (more easily than in times of peace) the important from that which is not important. Moreover, in 1945, we thought that the world had learned its lesson. We saw, very unrealistically perhaps, possibilities for a new world, so our new association (of graphic designers) was founded with a clear point of departure."

This new association was GKF, the Society of Graphic Designers, and rather than advertising designers or those involved with industry and commerce, many of its members were designers inclined toward a "leftist" political persuasion. The mainstream designers formed their own association called the VRI in 1948. The two associations did not get along – a situation that is typically Dutch. In one small village for example, it was possible to find a Protestant cycling club, a Roman Catholic cycling club, a Communist cycling club and a general cycling club. Special interest groups were sometimes divided along political or philosophical lines rather than religious ones.

During this period, graphic designers who belonged to the

GKF received many "cultural" assignments, such as catalogues, exhibition posters for museums, commissions from the PTT, the design of municipal exhibitions and other non-commercial projects. Small companies and printing firms were also becoming more interested in the new approach to design. In about 1950, the printing firm De Ijsel began producing a series of calendars which explored a different subject each year and were designed by GKF members Piet Klaase and Han de Vries.

Until the late 1950s, the development of graphic design in the Netherlands lagged behind that of other industrialized countries for the simple reason that money and technical materials were still scarce. At this time, the Dutch were quietly influenced by American life and culture, and Dutch designers regarded with both admiration and envy the graphics they saw from the Container Corporation of America and Olivetti (which had offices in the US as well as Italy). Furthermore, new production techniques like photo-typesetting and scanning, and new papers like Kromekote were only slowly introduced in the Netherlands, and they were not always greeted enthusiastically, since some graphic designers thought the new technology would harm the quality of their designs. Still, there were some forward-looking companies that supported graphic design. Among these were the wine merchants Oud in Haarlem, which had all their labels, catalogues and advertisements designed by Jan van Keulen; the international rayon industry AKU in Arnhem, where the magazine *Rayon Reveu* was designed by Otto Treumann; and the printing firm Drukkerij Meyer in Wormerveer, which produced technical books designed by such GKF designers as Dick Elffers and Jurriaan Schrofer. Steendrukkerij de Jong and Co. published the *Quadrat Prints*, which had an international reputation. The De Ploeg textile mills in Bergeyk were known both for employing the talents of distinguished graphic designers and for the superior design of their own products. The paint manufacturer Sikkens made an impact on the art world in general with its publications and by organizing symposia on color. These developments placed the Netherlands, in the early 1960s, among those countries in which graphic design was valued as a discipline in its own right and not simply considered – as it was elsewhere – a bastard child of fine art.

This respect for art and design is evident in the use of fine and applied art by the Netherlands postal and telecommunications service, an organization which, since the early 1930s, has had an office to oversee the development of its architecture, industrial design and graphic design, as well as the acquisition of fine art. Moreover, the example set by the PTT has led to new initiatives on the part of other firms.

The Netherlands state printing house is responsible for printing forms, brochures and books for all the government ministries.

J. van Krimpen, 1946

A B C D H I J K L O P Q R

Typeface 'Holland Mediæval',
S.H. de Roos, 1912

The former director of the state printing house, Th. Oltheten, saw in this responsibility an opportunity to have all such printing well designed and executed. Under his guidance, the design office has been able to produce a wide variety of distinguished visual communications.

Recently, Marjan Unger, an art critic and the wife of type designer Gerard Unger, stated at the opening of an exhibition that the Netherlands has more typeface designers per square kilometre than any other country in the world. This interest in type design seems to be part of the national character. Antwerp and Haarlem were historically centers of printing and type design. Before World War II there were two noted type designers, Jan van Krimpen, who worked for Johan Enschede & Zonen, and Sjoerd de Roos, who worked for Typefoundry Amsterdam. They, in turn, passed on their skills and interest to students like Sem Hartz and Dick Dooijes. The typographer and type designer Gerrit Noordzij also influenced a number of Dutch type designers.

In spite of the Dutch talent for typography and design, Dutch industry has sometimes shocked and insulted designers in the Netherlands by seeking its graphic solutions abroad. In the early 1960s, KLM, the Royal Dutch Airlines, asked the British designer F H K Henrion to redesign its corporate identity and develop a style manual, and more recently, after the merger of the ABN and Amro banks, the board of directors looked abroad to find a non-Dutch design group to create a house style. The Dutch international holding company AKZO also asked non-Dutch designers to design a symbol. It may be that these corporations look to England and the US rather than their homegrown talent because of a typical Dutch tendency to think that only foreign goods and services are worthwhile.

An exception is the Dutch firm DSM, the former Dutch State Mines, which developed into a powerful chemical producer. It needed an identity that would adapt to every aspect of its operations, from tramway cars to business forms and signs, and could be used in both its national and international divisions. In 1966, DSM asked me to be co-ordinator of a committee that would make recommendations for a design manual. The manual, which appeared in loose-leaf binder form, was enormously thorough in its detailing of the house style. Furthermore, because it reflected the concerns not only of designers, but also of industry executives, it was not simply style laid over existing material; rather, it responded to fundamental needs of the industry at large and served as a model for future corporate identity projects.

The 1960s also witnessed the formation of a number of independent design studios in the Netherlands. Total Design, a visual communications and design office founded by Kramer, Wissing, Box, Schwarz and Crouwel, was established in 1963.

Tel Design logo,
Netherlands Railways, 1946

BRS logo, Ministry of
Internal Affairs, 1967

(Originally a proponent of the use of formal typography, Total Design, under the guidance of Jelle van de Toorn Vrijthoff, has recently become a pioneer in the use of the Aestedes computer, an exceptionally versatile machine designed and developed in the Netherlands.) The very small office, BRS, was founded in 1969; and Tel Design, known for its signage projects, in 1962. (The latter's principal, Gert Dumbar, subsequently founded Studio Dumbar.)

The design offices on the "Hague circuit" are the PTT design office, the state printing house, Tel Design, and Studio Dumbar. This means that many assignments automatically stay within the Hague. Equally distinguished design offices, like BRS and Total Design, are located in Amsterdam.

In 1967, the Netherlands Railways asked Tel Design to create a total visual identity. This tremendous job had a successful outcome and from the early 1970s on, gave all the Dutch transportation services a completely fresh look. Because it was such an important and visible institution, the Netherlands Railways, by implementing a new corporate image, inspired other smaller institutions to follow its lead, as often happens in the Netherlands. Many bus companies throughout the country, for example, adopted a style similar in color-coding and pictogram design.

Also in 1967, a very important step was taken by one of the Netherlands ministries which would further the use of good design at all levels of Dutch government. The head of information services for the Ministry of Internal Affairs, Dick Houwaart, started looking for design groups other than that of the state printing house to solve visual communications problems in all divisions of that ministry, which was responsible for approximately thirty sub-institutions. With the support of Secretary General Dr P. van Dijke, Houwaart was able to solicit pitches from five design offices. The BRS office won the competition and subsequently worked with the design office of the state printing house to develop new design policies for the Ministry of Internal Affairs.

This far-reaching project, extending to all levels of state government, changed the public face of the Netherlands. As in the preparation of the DSM manual, the employees of the various institutions and departments of the ministry were involved in the analyses which preceded the proposal for a new house style. The result was the creation of new designs on the basis of need and functionalism rather than the application of a visual coating to existing designs. BRS was so organized that the commission to redesign the ministry's forms was given to a subdivision of BRS which specializes only in the legibility, use and development of forms. BRS recently also undertook the redesign of all Dutch tax forms, a project they will approach by first revising the language so that ordinary Dutch citizens can understand what they are asked to fill out. This is a remarkably courageous assignment for a

119

100-guilder note,
Ootje Oxenaar, 1977

GKf

Wim Crouwel, 1962

Nico Hey, 1969

government organization to give to a design studio. The premise that the design solution has to grow out of the function of the item being designed is the strength of the BRS office, which is today the largest design office in the Netherlands.

The BRS project was so successful that in the last fifteen years a number of Dutch institutions have been subjected to a complete renovation of official appearance. Everything from coins and bank notes to signage and timetables has been redesigned. The lion and coat of arms have been replaced with a simplified symbol. We have grown accustomed to this redesign, which has sometimes even gone too far, resulting in a plethora of abbreviations and logos that seem to have sacrificed individuality to economy of means.

A significant factor in the look of official graphic design in the Netherlands is sensitivity to signage and other graphics shown by the Office of the State Architect, which is responsible for the appearance of all government buildings. Although new buildings for ministries are constructed according to very strict guidelines, these allow for the introduction of appropriate visual material.

While BRS has designed, with some difficulty, the new identity for the Netherlands State Bank, Ootje Oxenaar has been given enormous freedom in designing Dutch bank notes. Two years ago, Oxenaar designed his last bank note, the 250-guilder note. His successor is Jaap Drupsteen. So far only Drupsteen's 25-guilder note has been issued. Drupsteen is mainly known for his television graphics, which created a completely new look in Dutch television. The official Netherlands technical assistance group for television not only has a studio for television graphics, but also employs individual designers like Drupsteen who have created some unique projects for Dutch television. However, the more extreme experiments, like those produced when Drupsteen was working for the Dutch company VPRO, are no longer seen.

In 1969, the two associations GKF and VRI buried their philosophical differences and decided to form one, stronger organization called the GVN. Of course, the result was that a few diehards did not wish to be a part of the new constellation. Furthermore, in the same year, Nico Hey, Bob McLarren and I founded the Art Directors Club Nederland. Nico Hey was the art director/co-owner of the advertising agency Hansen, Hey en Veltman. Bob McLarren was a well-known creative director, while I had just returned from New York from the post of chairman of the Visual Communications Department at Pratt Institute. The new era of the 1960s made new situations in the advertising world possible. Successful art directors claimed positions in agency management, while at the same time they formed the Art Directors Club in order to keep up with and solidify their power in the creative world. The founding of this club was not welcomed by the representatives of the old power structures within graphic

Vara Broadcasting,
Swip Stolk, 1977

'Murderous',
Gielijn Escher, 1988

design. An each-organization-for-itself attitude on the part of the GVN was the reason that all creative visual communication groups did not get together. It is only now, in 1991, that Dutch art directors and designers are beginning to exchange ideas and share professional activities. For the first time, the board of the Art Directors Club Nederland includes a member – Gert Dumbar – who represents the BNO association of graphic designers (formerly the GVN).

In 1970, I published a wall chart in Japan defining different groups of poster designers in the Netherlands. I depicted them under the headings "typographers", "designers", "graphic artists" and "humorous designers". Among the typographers at that time were only Willem Sandberg and Wim Crouwel; among the designers were Treumann, myself and Aart Verhoeven, as well as Jan van Toorn. Among the graphic artists were Dick Elffers, Nicolaas Wijnberg, and Jan Bons, while Dick Bruna with his humorous illustrations made up a separate group. Since then, Jan van Toorn has had a tremendous influence on the new generation of poster designers, like Anthon Beeke, for example, and also, to a certain extent, on Swip Stolk. Jan van Toorn could now be considered a unique designer who is not related to any group. His strong political philosophy and his striking way of expressing himself with collage make him one of the leading designers of posters. Crouwel has designed posters for the Stedelijk Museum in Amsterdam since 1970, but has retired somewhat from graphic design during his tenure as a director of the Boymans van Beuningen Museum in Rotterdam. Elffers, who was very active up to his death in 1990, has remained a strong influence, as has Jan Bons. Anthon Beeke, originally influenced by Van Toorn, has emerged as a strong poster designer. His posters for theatre and other cultural institutions, though beautiful in their own right, have been criticized because they fail to convey information. The posters of Gielijn Escher, on the other hand, are both visually striking and strong on information. This artist and typographer sometimes prints his remarkable posters himself, and sometimes has them silk screened.

Another substantial group of graphic designers, like Harry Sierman, Rick Vermeulen, Karel Martens and Walter Nikkels, work in the field of book and bookcover design for publishers like Arbeiderspers, De Bezige Bij, Querido, Van Oorschot, Sun and others. This group is very serious about their work. In Holland, it is rewarding to go to a good bookstore to see how the books are produced and displayed. Though one cannot always see the most expensive books, this is still a good way to discover unique examples of Dutch typography.

Finally, there are three important studios that should be mentioned. The first of these is Studio Dumbar. Principal Gert

Dumbar's comment, "Sometimes [other designers] think that I am an artist, and I am," serves as a basis for his philosophy and work. Dumbar introduced, principally for the Holland Festival, posters with staged photography. This technique had also been used much earlier by Piet Zwart for a cover of Film Monographs, published by Brusse in 1952. Dumbar and his photographer stage objects and printed matter, add coloured lights, and thus create new images. He then superimposes these images over and around his typographic message.

Another group which makes use of staged photography is Hard Werken, a Rotterdam-based studio including designers Rick Vermeulen and Gerard Hadders. A group of designers of leftist political philosophy has grown up around Rob Schröder.

The Netherlands offers its citizens unusual social support. From birth to death, the individual is protected and sometimes financially supported. This is also the case in the arts. Every municipality has, by law, funds to support the arts and gives grants where it is felt to be necessary. This generosity provides for exhibitions, musical performances, small festivals and similar cultural activities. There are additional grants to help make these happenings successful. It follows that the entrance fees to these performances are subsidized and that posters, invitations and catalogues are also paid for by subsidy. Owing to this practice, the competition between non-subsidized performances and subsidized performances is somewhat unfair. As mentioned above, GKF designers usually worked for the subsidized cultural events, while the VRI designers worked for advertising agencies, commerce and industry. This situation still exists in the Netherlands, and because of it, in official exhibitions and in books and design annuals, the work presented from the Netherlands is somewhat one-sided. The subsidized work, rather than the design for commerce and industry, is, by and large, that which is chosen for publication, and when viewers see it, they often say, "It looks very nice, but what is it for?"

Hard Werken (Hard at work), Gerard Hadders, Poster, 1980

MIMMO CASTELLANO

Italy

Graphic design in Italy: from the sixties to the eighties

Campo, 11/12, Italy, December 1982

This article, which was originally an interview given to the magazine *Campo* in 1982, holds a special place in my memory; at the time I had no idea how my words would be borne out by the turn of events twelve years later. It is worth adding that characters who have been able to work and pursue their professions profitably have naturally only been able to do so because they belonged to the right political party. For even longer than the deplored fascists and certainly with less historical far-sightedness than the fascists, they subjected the historical culture of Italian design to an interplay of patronage and power. Characters who did not toe the establishment line were inevitably put aside.

If Milan was the capital of Italian design, Craxi was the boss of the city. The prestigious "Compasso d'oro" award was given to the graphic designer who took care of the Italian Socialist Party's campaign.

The Lombard Regional Council or Milan City Council was quick to subsidize costly monographs for party sympathizers.

Graphic design contracts for the Milan-based RAI 3 TV company went to those whose loyalties lay with the Communists.

Contracts for the Triennale exhibition went to Socialists destined for the top, with design magazine editorships dangled as a carrot.

The unwritten law of the chosen few was to pass over or even boycott – as happened on several occasions – non-Socialist colleagues; in other words colleagues who could not face having to kowtow to the powers that be – powers that history has shown to be common criminals.

What I wrote at that time has been confirmed by the *Mani pulite* bombshell. All this scandal has sadly proved a huge disaster for Italian design. It marked a historical lull in a culture now lost to us for good.

Milan, 18 July 1994

When one leaves after fifteen years of trying, striving, trusting, daily commitment, defeats, illusory victories, one leaves because there is really no alternative.

At least for one who chooses to carry out his profession in a civil context; one who wishes to express himself and his profession

123

without having to worry about stepping out of line.

In Southern Italy, the pressure to toe the line is always insistent and overbearing, vulgar and arrogant. Southern Italy has unfortunately remained over-fond of its ignorance, its lack of culture and above all of its refusal to learn.

For years, the South has turned out centurions of power who parade their coarseness before the entire nation, and have the nerve to congratulate themselves for it. It is enough to flick through the pages of newspapers from the last few months – or even the last few years or the last few decades.

If anything, the phenomenon has sadly become even worse, particularly during the last few months.

Even though I have now left Southern Italy, I unfortunately still keep in touch and I still, again unfortunately, continue to harbour an unspoken and secret hope that there is still time to change.

Now, at the end of 1982, after being affectionately pressed by you at *Campo* to produce yet another overview of the situation, I frankly feel bound to admit that my hopes have absolutely no foundation in truth. There is an explanation, and it is clear for all to see: the men of power are always there, immortal, for decades, in the newspapers, in regional government, in town councils, in the places that are supposed to be our centres of learning: universities, schools, academies. Hopes may be aroused because, for example, a new school is opened – yet the reins of this great power will always be held by the puppet masters through their puppets, who are usually incompetent but always faithful servants. The choices are limited in this bleak situation: toe the line or you are out. By this I mean that unless you have sufficient independent means to remain free of the authorities, or unless you put up with or even endorse their crookedness by putting your professionalism at their service, or unless you open a restaurant (if they let you), you may as well pack your bags.

On a personal level, I can say that I was fortunate enough to stand up to the Bari authorities for fifteen years because almost all my customers were companies belonging to the IRI (Institute for Industrial Reconstruction). During the golden period of this now stricken organization, such companies realized a need to project an image of extremely good form and taste. During all those years, therefore, I worked in Bari for the RAI, ENI, Italsider, Alitalia and INA. Then everything collapsed with the ill-fated arrival of the centre-left. On the day the Socialists arrived in the city hall (1962) they began the inexorable process of dividing everything up among themselves, thus contaminating all sectors of Italian life. I am entitled to say this because I was virtually a Socialist myself in those days.

All state-run companies were controlled by the DC (Christian Democrats). Even though I was known to be a subversive, with a file on my activities at the police station, I could still be trusted to organize an exhibition, a book or a newspaper campaign.

Yet when my friends reached the city hall, all possibility of work literally vanished.

Open the door to Sinisgalli's room in the ENI tower at Eur – the same room where I planned the "Paese Lucano" project with Sinisgalli and Mattei – and you would find Giovacchino Albanese sitting there. You simply had to excuse yourself for opening the wrong door and close it again.

At that point, I had no further reason to stay in the South. The importance lay not in the fact of going to Milan or New York but in the fact of leaving the South.

When one speaks of business culture, one does not realize that the biggest business in Southern Italy is the State, operating through its myriad party-controlled organizations. Business cannot therefore be understood in the same sense. We are faced with a huge cover-up, a changing of labels, because the vessel that should contain the State contains the parties, while the one that should contain the parties is empty.

I was a child of the future during the Second World War when the work of rebuilding Italy began. But I believe that we are in a worse situation today. No one has yet realized that we must begin to rebuild the conscience of the people – and this does not apply solely to the South. The South has ended up by contaminating all Italy, the Southern mentality has reached such heights because a prevalently Southern political class has dominated the Italian scene unopposed. The results are plain for all to see. How can we continue to hope for a nation that after twenty years offers us the same Prime Minister as we had in 1962, instead of the first lay government we have succeeded in voting in – for our sins – during our forty years as a Republic. We certainly cannot be taken seriously as a people if we allow ourselves to be taken in by superficial considerations and give our backing to Pertini. He may be one of the best presidents we have ever had in this unfortunate country, but we are forgetting that in his memoirs Nenni remembers him as a mischievous rogue who used to go and fire off rounds under the windows of the Savoys when they were about to go into exile. And he was certainly old enough to know better at the time.

One objection that could be raised against my replies to your questions is that I over-politicize my subject. Unfortunately we cannot deny the situation of national malaise so firmly rooted in Southern Italy, that exporter of sickness, patronage, mafia, *camorra* – and boorish politicians who have turned this country into a laughing stock.

What sense would there by in setting up a school in Salerno, Bari or Palermo? We could certainly do it, but only if we imported

125

public officials from Switzerland, for example.

Education is directly influenced by the State and society. In the words of Arbasino, what would be the point with this State and this society?

In a world where all forms of communication, including visual communication, are instantly available in all corners of the globe, it is difficult to speak of ethnic roots and cultural components because these are becoming increasingly diluted in anthropological terms. These days you can find a girl with a short skirt and dyed hair in a tiny place like Vomero or in Piccadilly Circus. This does not prevent anyone who still possesses any kind of ethnic background from letting it overflow into their work to reach a wider or even international audience.

Is there still place for hope in such a gloomy situation? Even in my blackest moods, I still hope a thunderbolt will strike the "palazzo" one day.

KEN CATO

Australia

One Designer's Manifesto

Communication Arts Advertising Annual, USA, December 1994

For some time I have been agonizing over the possible content of this article. There are so many issues that need addressing. On the assumption that many of the readers of this publication are designers, I would like to take this opportunity to address some issues which I feel are hampering the growth and understanding of our profession. Although I am probably too old to be naïvely optimistic, I have a very positive view of the potential of design. It is still a young profession, driven by passion, ego, creativity and the desire to produce exciting, ground-breaking work. Most designers know the work being done in their own countries and internationally. They are aware of the work and practices of the leading design firms and high profile individuals. That's good – up to a point. But I believe that we have become perversely introspective. We have become obsessed with the icons of our awards. There is a plethora of award-giving organizations, publications and competitions.

Gone are the days when winning an award was a rare opportunity and that those who won really deserved recognition. I used to believe that national and international awards gave us all an opportunity to view the best on offer, continually raise the standards and therefore stimulate better work from our studios and ourselves. But award annuals are no longer showing the cream of design – what we are getting is fat-free milk! I have started to doubt the purpose of these shows and the type of work they encourage. It seems to me that the objective should not only encompass the areas already expressed but that it should send a message of encouragement to the industry leaders: a message that design is not only a way for them to have their organizations look better, but also a way to communicate more effectively and gain higher recall and respect in the minds of those they address, and ultimately have a positive effect on the bottom line. This seems logical until you analyse the content of some of the major design shows. For example, over a thirteen-year period one award show accepted entries that comprised over 50 per cent of designers' self-promotion and stationery pieces, or work for paper companies, printers and other companies communicating services for designers. This balance is not uncommon.

127

MELBOURNE
1996

Melbourne's bid to host
the 1996 Olympic Games
in Australia coincided with
the 100th anniversary of
the Olympics.

As I write, another list of award show winners has come across my desk, proudly announcing that the major winner has won two awards for work produced for his own studio. Where is the great award-winning work created for clients?

Is it because as designers we think the only high standard work we do is for ourselves? I am aware of shows that emphasize the performance of design. But what we do is not an end in itself; it is always coupled with other influences. I believe we need to communicate the profession's values and worth to the business community, and recognize the corporations who use design as a significant factor in the development of their products, corporate culture and communications. Maybe then designers won't need the self-congratulating ego boost of nefarious awards: the bottom line might be enough.

Design expenditure is rarely reflected on the corporate balance sheet. It is concealed by other components of the corporation. But in most cases the organization's "design expenditure" is far greater than any one executive ever contemplates. Product development, stationery, corporate print, packaging, transport livery, retail outlets, building architecture, interior design, signage, uniforms and corporate wardrobe are all part of integrated design. However, individual managers ordering their separate elements focus on getting their jobs done rather than assessing overall coordination with other components. Without a central design policy, a random approach to design can create confusion in the market-place by projecting different visual identities.

It is quite possible that an organization may have a dozen managers ordering different design components. Each of these managers may be very good at their own tasks, but without overall coordination the opportunity to create a positive, cumulative effect is lost. By harnessing that opportunity a company can generate enormous image power. It is not until a level of excellence is reached, with each individual design component and its relationship established within the identity's broader visual language, that the true value of design can be appreciated.

Businesses are becoming increasingly aware of the number of aspects which are affected by design, but they still often underestimate the overall amount of money being spent on design-driven components. Hopefully, comprehensive design strategies will become an increasingly recognized ingredient in successful business management. The visual message transcends language and cultural barriers. It is essential to global communications. It is no longer an option. Companies must take control of the visual components of their businesses.

As designers we all need to know our clients' requirements. We must really listen – not just to what is said in a brief, but to what isn't said. Design is a commodity which needs to be sold to companies; we need to educate clients on how to select and buy it. Unless we start talking up our profession and those in it, we will not improve our credibility. In most cases the purchase of design has not been part of managers' training. Buying design for the first time demands insight, judgment and an understanding of the profession.

Most business courses do not recognize design as an essential and effective marketing tool. The average client is taught marketing, accounting, research techniques and business law, but very few have experience in the purchase of design. A manager needs to know how to select a design company that is best suited to their needs and to ask specific questions: how much to pay for the work; how to judge the work; how to have a meaningful working relationship with the designer; how to effectively brief a project to the designers; how to assess the performance; and how ultimately to make a designer a valuable part of the marketing team.

I have often thought about the frightening position that clients find themselves in when they decide to work with a designer. In most cases it is buying the unknown. They cannot visualize the finished result for which they are committed to paying, in their minds, exorbitant amounts of money. It's not often in this life that we make purchases sight-unseen, yet we expect our clients to trust us implicitly and accept the situation without so much as a murmur. I am certainly not suggesting we do speculative work, but I do think we should consider the justifiable fears and trepidation of our potential clients.

The city decorations included a series of large, freestanding metal structures depicting athletes engaging in a variety of sports. The surfaces were painted in the bright primary colours of the symbol, and spattered many times with "anti-graffiti" paint.

Those few companies that understand design are known and appreciated by us all but they are not in the majority; the rest need help in making their design expenditures more effective. The money is already committed and being spent; getting a cumulative result is the real potential bonus. As designers, I believe our goals should be very clear: to promote, nurture and give value to the profession of graphic design; and to encourage, support and recognize quality work. It is up to us to evaluate the profession of graphic design and the value of the aesthetics of design within the community, thereby improving the visual standards and expectations of our society. Satisfying the ego will come naturally.

Designers must become powerful enough individually and collectively to persuade decision-makers that good design is good business – and good for society. The question is always, what is quality work? Part of design is function, although function can vary widely for different problems and audiences. The aesthetic part of design is subjective; however, all too often we are surrounded by retail stores, housing estates, government buildings and offices that reflect anonymous bad design. The long-term success of the design industry will surely depend upon its ability to increase the value of design within the culture and fabric of society.

As a profession generally, designers place appallingly little value on their work. We do not seem confident enough to realize that clients should be choosing the optimum solution to their problems, or implementing the best design program, rather than deciding on the lowest price. We *do* have unique skills. Most of us have a long-term commitment to making design a recognized and valued profession. No matter what the cost, it is the quality of the work that is important.

Design is not just an art: it is a business. It is about time designers learned the art of business. It is ludicrous to think that one does not affect the other. A designer may choose not to manage his business personally but that is no excuse for poor business management. The more effectively a business is run, the more professional it will appear to be to clients, and the more valuable its design products will become.

We also have a further responsibility to encourage quality design whether it be with conventional practising designers or with those who are working in more experimental areas. I also believe that the profession has an obligation to look to the education and development of our younger designers. There is an abundance of talent but we need to guide its development. It appears that most design colleges look to educate and develop students to become freelance designers – the one man band! The number of businesses with under ten people seemingly supports this theory. While this approach has its merits, it does develop a cottage industry mentality, and doesn't prepare young designers to work as part of a team – either as a member of a design team or in a relationship with a person or corporation who has real need of their skills. Most projects we aspire to are the product of client/designer relationships, and larger teams of people to implement the concept. Unlike art college, we do not have to do it all ourselves. Everyone is in search of the genius: employer, client and colleague. But in reality they only come along every so often. In the meantime, there are many highly talented and skilled individuals who could make a valuable contribution and exceed their own personal abilities if they were able to function as part of a team.

Designers are also at risk of becoming production managers. The real problem is not that the computer is taking over, it is that the skills base is dying out. While I understand that there is a new computer language, in most cases the technology is used as a tool and nothing more. Too many design courses have insufficient funds to afford state-of-the-art equipment, or sufficient time to teach the new technology in addition to the more traditional art and design skills, let alone the business of design. It is essential that design management and understanding the value of design become part of business courses. It will take work on both sides if we are to see improvement in the understanding and use of design.

Design is an exciting profession, and the opportunity to share knowledge and experience can only make design more valuable. Good design is universal. Good design is good design regardless of subjective judgments. It is therefore crucial to care about the integrity of the work and the industry and to nurture those who will inherit it.

GERT DUMBAR

Netherlands

Room for chance

Vormberichten 4, 1994

I am going to talk about the role of governments and private clients in the development of graphic design. Such words imply a number of things. As they are stated, we seem hedged in by authority. With our record of service we now deserve better. Our game (I prefer that to the word "role") with governments and private clients results in an uneasy relationship. A LAT ("Living Apart Together") relationship. To keep it exciting, and that is what is important in a LAT relationship, we must not strive too much for harmony or symbiosis because that leads nowhere. Where the practical side of the relationship allows – and that is not unimportant in a LAT relationship – we would do better to play strictly. That prevents disappointment.

I accept that the term "private clients" refers to business. Entrepreneurs. There are two types of entrepreneurs, as you can read in any book on this subject. Some entrepreneurs are primarily concerned with making a profit and secondly in ensuring the continuity of their business. They are the conservatives. With progressives it is exactly the opposite. Between them all shades are possible.

Our other type of client, governments, are institutions which on the one hand take in money, currently about 60 per cent of our national income, and on the other hand give out money – if they do it properly, in the interests of everyone. That's how simple it is.

Entrepreneurs and governments have to act in a way which serves the purposes or at least the interests of customers and subjects, because otherwise they soon cease to be entrepreneurs or governments, as history, particularly recent history, has shown. Thus, besides their accountants, business advisers, police and security service, they also need us. And now I will be serious. Every client, entrepreneur or government gets exactly the graphic designer he deserves. A question of live and let live in the LAT relationship. You are only as good a graphic designer as your client lets you be. Incidentally, the opposite is also true. In such a LAT relationship the designer is kept on a leash. Across the surface of the earth blows the bitter wind of monoculture – where you can still talk about a culture at all – because every surprise has been eliminated.

The purpose of the business is generally reduced to making a profit, and no one talks about continuity any more. And everyone is surprised that the business and the LAT relationship is doing badly.

Graphic design in the Netherlands begins roughly with Jan Toorop with his "salad oil logo", developed around the turn of the century and still well-known. We view this with admiration but we never let it be forgotten that without the visionary Jan van Marken, director of the Gist en Spiritusfabriek in Delft, the Nederlandse Oliefabriek (later Calvé) would never have had such a salad oil logo. Unfortunately I cannot say much more about van Marken since that would need extra words. A personality who allowed his graphic adviser – and all other advisers – personality. No! Who demanded it. Of course, the same can be said about J F van Royen who, in the second decade of this century, laid the foundations, through the PTT, of our elegant and meticulous government communications system which the civilized world envies; the rest of them think it's rubbish. This was also said, and sometimes still is, about the "salad oil logo".

Here I would also like to mention Kees van der Leeuw, director of Van Nelle, a remarkable man, who was painting in Egypt when his family thought he was learning the cotton trade in Hamburg. And he was a composer too. In the 1920s he made sure that the finest factory in the Netherlands was built for Van Nelle and that Jacques Jongert designed a company logo which was unprecedented at that time. Later van der Leeuw financed the Krishnamurti movement, became a psychiatrist in Vienna, played an enormous part in the rebuilding of Rotterdam after the war and was Chairman of the Board of Curators of the Technical University in Delft.

As I said, the few clients who really played a part in the development of our profession rarely found designers who could keep pace with them.

Such clients tolerate in us something which in fact they can scarcely tolerate: uncertainty – something which both entrepreneurs and governments (particularly governments) detest. I am speaking about creativity, real creativity: the leap into the unknown. And although the result of the uncertain outcome of the creative adventure may be better than expected, this still remains the most delicate aspect of the LAT relationship which entrepreneurs pursue with us and vice versa.

I want to link creativity with something known as *serendipity*, which means to find something that you haven't been looking for but which changes everything that went before and comes after. The English word *serendipity* was coined by Horace Walpole (1717-97), who used it for the first time in 1754 in a letter. Walpole described the adventures of the Three Persian Princes of Serendip. "By chance and shrewdness they discovered things which they were not looking for." They looked for one thing and found another.

They were very surprised about this themselves. That is creativity in our profession.

In 1957 Robert Merton gave the following definition of *serendipity:* "The phenomenon of serendipity refers to the fairly common experience of an unanticipated, abnormal and strategic fact which provokes a new theory or the extension of an existing theory."

To cut a long story short, the discovery of an error – this should reassure clients – by which the system is changed out of all recognition as if by magic or with the passage of time.

Serendipity, as described by Walpole and Merton, and practised by Van Marken, Van Royen and Van der Leeuw, is the salvation of the routine in our profession. Because we should not delude ourselves, there is naturally something inherently routine in our profession. It is extremely closely bound to culture and the most powerful streams flow fast. Despite barriers against retrospective exhibitions there is only a thin wall dividing the fervour of the Russian Revolution from the later Soviet propaganda, Bauhaus from the Nazi substitute, and the Swiss Style from the sterile trash which the consumer society had to, and still has to, put up with. It is up to us, as the ears and eyes of our clients, always to think of something new. Because otherwise, by too much of the good and therefore in fact too little, nothing is good any more. What then follows is the unimaginative piling up of bad and poorly executed clichés: the disastrous end of any style which becomes a mannerism. The wood through which you can no longer see the trees. Through which nothing more is communicated. Then you have to get to work with an axe and you've got to do some heavy weeding and hacking to bring light into the design forest. To use a more obvious metaphor, we must keep open the wells from which we drink. Otherwise they will silt up. We are not servants but water carriers. That is how we must conduct ourselves. That is not only our duty, that is our function in its entirety.

It is very tempting to give an example of *serendipity* from our own practice and I am very happy to do so. The PTT company logo of 1989 was firstly a very simple logo, with three primary colours for the different tasks, adapted in a variety of forms. Then the forms derived from that logo suddenly began to take the most unexpected turns on our drawing boards. You could also say that they tried to run away with us. We could have immediately put a stop to them, but we did not want to do that. We gave them more or less free rein – and of course the exact measurement of that "more or less" is important. So a logo emerged within the company logo of PTT with innumerable derived forms, but always identifiable as "PTT", right down to the crockery. The most widely stolen crockery in the Netherlands. We saw every stolen cup or saucer as a compliment to the freedom which our client gave us.

Where do we find the clients who allow us our unexpected, unimaginable serendiptic brainwaves? I have read the annual report of the unusually successful company Steenkolen Handels Vereniging (SHV); its profit for 1991 was over 500 million guilders. That annual report contained a fragment from, I think, the second maxim of the *Tao Te Ching* of Lao-tzu: "... working without doing and difficult tasks are done as if they are easy." This recalls the "new realism" of the 1960s; no wonder that Total Design even then had involved the writers Vaandrager and Sleutelaar in developing a new company logo for SHV. A slim volume is circulating in this company in which the corporate philosophy says the following with reference to the method: 1. look for the unusual, 2. motivate people, 3. listen, learn and respect, 4. keep things simple. That too reads like a poem by Vaandrager.

Elsewhere, the Chairman of SHV, Paul Fentener van Vlissingen, describes the management structure of the Catholic Church as an example to multinational concerns; the church is a multinational which has existed for 2000 years, "with only five management structures from priest to Pope".

There you have it. That is how simple things can be. If our clients thought like that they would be able to take real pleasure in our work. We are ready for it.

Our world is full of official and overcoded semiotics and has to a large extent succumbed to it. Sometimes there is a ray of light – Fentener van Vlissingen and Freddy Heineken too. In a controversial interview in NRC-Handelsblad he rejected the unmanageable megastructure of a United Europe with a population of 500 million. The occasion for the interview was a booklet in which the realist Heineken put forward the idea of dividing the future United Europe pragmatically into seventy-five small states on the American model. Arranged, not according to nationalism or patriotism, but honourable chauvinistic sentiment. Just as the historical *Bos Atlas* showed what Europe had always looked like. And we can investigate this further in the work of the French historian-anthropologist Emmanuel Todd. There are indeed stronger, more hygienic, more legitimate and therefore more inspiring associations possible than the ogre which hangs over our heads.

FRANCO GRIGNANI

Italy

Symbols' language for our age

Foto & Dintorni, Rome, Tor Vergata University, 1st March 1994

Although our graphics profession is essentially derived from painting, this "source" has made us forget somewhat the visualizing function of our work.

"Visualizer", in the general sense of the word, is therefore a neologism, which expresses the task of a graphic artist looking for signs and symbols capable of making themselves visible. If we enter a landscape and we want to find out why some signs attract us more than others, we will see the lines of flight of perspectives, lines filled with apparent motion and strong contrasts.

As graphic artists, we give the message "everything to be seen" and "everything to be felt", but our physical and material means are almost always normal – the sign, the composition, the illustration – unless our eye is trained to see the tensive radial lines between the edges and the visual point of interest between the sign and the surface containing it.

What is this tension? It is a physical discomfort that is felt on traces of physical forces, on illusions and stimuli. Why does an arrangement of lines converging on a point have a disturbing hypnotic power over us? Why does a succession of lines with different radii give us the illusion of apparent motion? In years of research, I have been able to produce about 15,000 experiments on these questions which, unfortunately, apart from a few applied tests, are still in my cupboards. This vast theoretical experiment seems to me to see a contribution of stimulus and physical communication in the future of graphic art.

Our design is not in a frame, is not alone on a wall, but lives in printing, a space between so many competing spaces; it lives on the walls along roads, squeezed in and competing with other advertisements, other signs, other colours. Our small or large space cannot be submerged, but has to preserve its pulsating and communicative "image wave" that makes it live an almost physical life.

Are we still artists at this point? Creativeness and technique take over and change the means, the images and the sensations, acting physiologically on the human eye, not as an aesthetic enchantment but as motion, sound, sense of touch. These experiments are not

Ieri è nata la Optical Art e l'ha annunciata la rivista americana LIFE del 28 dicembre scorso. In questo spazio, ogni mese e da anni, Alfieri & Lacroix propone problemi visuali in un'area adattissima: la grafica. Alfieri & Lacroix è viva e moderna, ai problemi di comunicazione associa la più razionale e completa organizzazione per la stampa di qualità.

Advertising for Alfieri & Lacroix
Typography in Milan 1965

intended to solve merely theoretical problems because, when applied to portrayal, these principles can create a larger-than-life image, influence the size of a photograph, change the fabric of a drawing starting with other proportions.

We should recall that communication is always a dynamic fact and that it has a sense of apparent life. The eye is more sensitive to these phenomena and the brain takes more interest in them.

This research has been conducted starting from drawings made with geometric order. When distorting factors take over, their relationship is not destroyed but is refilled with more palpitating and living relationships or, when tension takes over, the development of the image spreads over the surfaces creating physical discomfort for the observer. The means are always drawn from the visual, because, with its laws, the mathematics of curvature, lenses and distances always produces a real image; it is a reality not within the laws of the human eye, and that makes it more intense.

Research has been conducted on the following subjects: dispersion of the centre; graphic hypnosis or induction; graphic tension; kinetics of the sign with a portrayal without a centre of visual interest; suggestion of musical tempos, particularly syncopated.

At present, what is different about advertising alongside the news? Often, owing to a certain ambiguity, the advertisement is confused with the rest of the paper, but this cunning cannot adjust to the problems of our world to which we are most committed throughout the large advertising organization.

What about education? Obviously, rather than "doing", we are trying to teach how "to see", as our profession has no poor or rich relations but is *unique* and wonderful.

137

HERBERT W. KAPITZKI

Germany

Ethics and commitment in design

Visuelle Gestaltung, 1993
(prepared for AGI Congress, Blois, 1990, but not delivered)

Whenever a worker experienced in the visual field is asked about his ethical or moral principles, he is taken aback. It is difficult for him to answer, particularly at this point in the century, when we are acutely aware that all moral values have become more confused than ever before.

An ethics that will serve to provide a designer with moral principles is far too complicated to be globally serviceable. It is obvious that communications which claim informational purposes will be based on elements very different from those used in advertisements, which have to be persuasive rather than explanatory and instructive.

In evaluating this matter, it also has to be decided whether design is one of the fine arts, or whether it is a functional aesthetic organization of communication. The moral attitude of the designer when he takes on a job, which is his means of existence, is assessed on a very different scale of values. Ethics as a philosophical science, the scrutinizing of principles and postulates of valuation, has always been left to philosophers, from Aristotle to Kant and Wittgenstein and others. If a designer talks about ethics or morals, he will do so on the basis both of his work - which is the fulfilment of somebody else's objectives - and of his own convictions; he will be influenced by his own experiences, the conditions of everyday life, and by his character. His own living conditions will always depend on the social conditions around him. The designer will be influenced in his behaviour by ethical considerations, but even more by the ethics of success. He is sentenced to be successful. If he is not successful, he cannot realize his own moral requirements.

This dialectic of design, between success and moral demands, has many consequences.

Visual design means the production of signs. Signs are not necessarily unequivocal; they can be interpreted in different ways. The production of signs is subject to social change. Changes depend on the *Zeitgeist*. That means that ethical and moral values are not fixed for all time.

I experienced this very clearly in my day-to-day work. In the l950s, it was quite exciting to work for an enterprise that made

138

Poster, client "Deutsche
Lufthansa"

special demands. Olivetti, Pirelli, IBM and Lufthansa, too, were
clients who felt even then that culture was a part of progress.

Propaganda, at that time, was something left over from the
1930s, though it helped some people in finding their direction;
marketing strategies had not yet been invented; corporate identity
was a matter of branding techniques; the Ulmer Hochschule für
Gestaltung had only recently been set up. At that time, when I was
trying to find my way, worrying whether I was sufficiently well-
prepared for the job and trying to define my standpoint, I was
commissioned to design a series of posters for Lufthansa. I decided
that it would be in the language of signs rather than illustrated.
The poster for the United States, for example, did not show the
Stars and Stripes, or typical landscapes, or similar images. I chose
the Statue of Liberty as an iconic sign. Like the rest of the series,
this icon stands on a ground showing the relevant country or
continent presented as a linear structure.

My idea was to find a form of presentation which carried
the contents in as concise a shape as possible. This probably did
not work very well in some cases, but it was the best I could do
at the time.

Recently, a book was published in Germany called *Stark für
die Freiheit* - "Strongly Pro-Freedom" - in which my poster was
classified, along with others, as political. This shows that any
commission which becomes public can be interpreted as a socio-
political statement, even if it originates from a business strategy. Its
original meaning may be perverted into the contrary: in this case,
into a metaphor for imperialism. The symbol of freedom becomes
a fetish of capitalist exploitation.

When I designed and produced the series of posters, neither
myself nor my client intended any hint of political message. You
could say that an equivocal sign had been introduced. In any case,
no tendentious form of information was intended.

I know that in Germany today there is an acute sensitivity
towards political matters, due to our permanently bad conscience
and our "profundity" as well; nevertheless, moral claims and
interpretations may change. It is beyond question, however, that
we must have a system of rules and values that serve as supra-
individual standards for treating our fellow people, even if it varies
from nation to nation as to how strictly they are followed. A poor
region cannot afford the moral values that a rich, industrialized
nation should observe. As Brecht put it, first comes food and then
come morals.

These ethical-moral requirements are linked to the question
of commitment in graphic design. Over the past forty years I have
learnt that commitment is always influenced by the exigencies of
the designers' work. I know of many colleagues who would love
to work for the improvement of ecological conditions in our

technological world, but who cannot do so because they must work for clients whose attitudes towards such problems are far from critical. They are forced to be opportunistic because their existence as designers depends on providing a service. I know what I am talking about here. That is why I try to argue as coolly as possible, since I know how hard it is to strike an exemplary attitude and stick to it.

The client should be asked to think again about his requirements, instead of the designer having to show more courage in his convictions. It is the client who should be motivated towards more commitment, not the designer. There are such clients in existence, and I have happily had experience of them. Let me mention one example. Some years ago I was designing the corporate information media for a Stuttgart daily newspaper. At one time there was a push by advertising agencies, trying to expand the use of their new methods and stopping at nothing. Anybody who wanted to keep his place in the market had to ask himself whether he was going to join the circus, or not. At this time, I was asked to design some advertisements and small posters. I was using a different visual language, concise and suggestive, as opposed to the language that was customary in the 1960s.

It goes without saying that there was a great struggle with both the publishers and the editorial staff. A newspaper works on a daily basis; signs that were coded seemed to disconcert them. My client – the publishers as well as the editors – eventually supported my kind of information media, and showed the depth of commitment necessary to the task. It was a very important experience for me, finding that it was possible to have congenial partners and to carry through an idea.

It became a great success for the newspaper, if not commercially at least on the level of ideas. This method of transmitting a visual message by including simple but precise texts became an historical event in newspaper publishing.

What it represents is a way of designing that is committed to community solidarity, and it serves the addressee better than a universe of exuberant, uncontrolled images and ideas. The work seems to show what has been lost over the years: a visual design of our surroundings reduced to the essentials, so to speak. Less is more.

P.S. This was written to be delivered at the AGI conference at Blois, May 1990. I have to say that we will never achieve the above aims if the media we found in our Blois hotel rooms is any indication. If we are calling for solidarity, this applies equally to our own way of presenting signs. There is no solidarity in using the picture of a mutilated female breast, in an ugly visual presentation, to make any statement whatsover. This discriminates against women. Someone who uses such an image starts from different ethical premises and his ethical attitude is already distorted.

140

LAURENCE MADRELLE

France

For a close relationship in the fight against Aids

French Agency for combating Aids
(AFLS=Agence francaise de lutte contre le sida)

I am a graphic designer, which needs some explanation. I have a certain conception, a certain practice in the creation of words associated with images. This responsibility imposes, in my view, recourse to collective means of expression and diffusion. I experience a feeling of aesthetic and ethical demands which are never satisfied.

A horizon pushed back further and further.

Finally, I have a certain attitude in relation to time, the lifespan of complex images, of systems of signs.

In brief, the feeling of an obligation in relation to the resulting meaning.

No help is too precious in this approach: such as that of writers, philosophers, sociologists who clarify our practices.

Thus, according to Roland Barthes, who I would like to quote in the circumstances which have brought me to speak to you today: "Language is a legislation, the style (*la langue*) is the code. We do not see the power in the style because we forget that any style is a classification and that any classification is oppressive. The style, as the performance of any language, is neither reactionary nor progressive; it is quite simply fascist; because fascism is not the prevention of speaking, it is the obligation to speak. As soon as it is proffered, even in the most profound intimacy of the subject, the style falls within the service of power." This is taken from his "Leçon inaugurale au Collège de France".

Our work (I say "our" because everything which I accomplish takes place only within an alchemy of beings, of knowledge, of experiences, of the wills of those around me) is distinguished from that of advertising in that, in particular, which places them under the sign of everyday life, and long lifespan.

The cause which unites us is a good subject in that it merits attention and requires the assistance of the best that our personal and professional experiences have been able to teach us.

We believe that it is necessary to listen more and better to the people (and not the targets) to whom our communicative objects address themselves, that it is necessary to devote ourselves to more investigations, finer, than in any other case in order to conceive the

Covers of the collection of little books for the homosexual community

written forms, the images, the associations of both together, in order to work our effects with greater care.

We must end up with durable artifacts, each of which has a particular mission to fulfil with those for whom they are intended.

Their format, their weight, the succession of words, illustrations, photos, colours...there is not one detail which escapes the filter of shared questioning, not one choice which is not made scrupulously, before our essential and irreducible part of creative pleasure comes into play.

It is without doubt there, at the crossroads of our desires and fears as well as our doubts, in our accumulated experiences, that we should seek what informs the practice of our work.

Among all the prevention messages, these few small books are only one among many possible words.

ENZO MARI

Italy

Why an exhibition of scythes?

Exhibition catalogue text, 1989

An exhibition of scythes? Yes. Because they are very beautiful. To me they are very beautiful even though, like everyone, when I was young I used to be frightened by the baroque image of Old Father Time. Naturally, I do not use the word beautiful in the hedonistic sense, but because I believe the scythe is a model of what design ought to be.

I think it is worth remembering that there are two ways of talking about design. The first refers somehow or other to the success of the Italian line, to companies that produce income for all, and to those "creatives" who find a gratifying work space that fits into the advertising agencies' national-popular vision. The second refers to the ideal sphere, to a serene reflection on the conditions and reasons for this work.

Cynically the "banal" is pleaded for; "decoration" is fostered, in the ignorance of its textual meaning as a reiteration of value; salvation is claimed, with cardboard triangles and tubes as silly metaphors for tympana and columns, the parody of a superficial and muddled memory. Not to mention those who persevere in the form-function philosophy, without realizing that, normal functions having ceased to exist, we are now in the parallel universe of Kitsch functions. And hovering over all this is the feeble aspiration to sculpture-objects.

This state of creative and productive obsession has led to a total expiry of the demand for design. Even those who possess a design culture – and there are some – fail to express it. And when, even if in acrobatic ways, they do achieve quality results, they appear to be of no influence. They are swept away by the sea of redundancy.

This state of affairs stems perhaps from the fact that, in an increasingly parcelled world, design is forced to lean on three cultures, of which a laughable synthesis is attempted: artistic research, technological research, and relations with industry, i.e. needs.

The formal quality of art (from Phidias to Duchamp) is the expression of the ideal of a society or of its contestation. The formal quality of technology (from the boomerang to Edison's electric light bulb) – of equal value to that of art – is the expression of the reasons of matter.

143

The formal quality of relations with industry (from Chartres cathedral to the Shakers) derives from the collective knowledge that permeates a society.

Let us now turn to one or two reflections on how the three cultures ought correctly to interact in design. In the first place, articles for living must respond effectively to their primary function. But ritual functions also can exist. Only on two conditions: that a recognizable rite exists; that the signs confirming the ritual are elements constituting a code.

It follows that design is founded essentially on the culture of technology and on that of relations with industry. If this is clear, it will also be understood why design must be related to the culture of art, though certainly not in an imitative way, since in that case it is degraded to applied art. The formal quality of art reappears – as the expression of the ideal of a society – since the correct use of technology strictly correlated to the transformation of relations with industry (and remember, also in the sense of needs) can be assumed as the sole ideal prospect for our society.

Going back to our scythes and to why they are beautiful, the first reason for their beauty lies in the type of need. It is a primary need: life or death. The survival of the peasant has always been tied to a thread, even to that of a scythe. The designing of this implement had necessarily to be perfect. The guarantee of perfection is afforded by the joint participation in the design process by the two depositaries of the cultures of reference mentioned: the reasons of technology expressed by the blacksmith, and the reasons for the need expressed by the peasant.

Let us see what are the needs to which technology has responded. The scythe has to be as inexpensive as possible (peasants have always been poor); it has to be very efficient indeed (very solid and very light: the tiring movement of reaping continues from dawn till dusk); the peasant must be able to maintain the efficiency of the implement by himself (frequently sharpening it with a whetstone and periodically by careful hammering).

Such are the basic general needs, to which a number of other, specific, variously interrelated needs can be added. These have been the cause of minor variations in shape or size and arise from such factors as: the characteristics of the land (plain, hill, steep, stony, etc.); the type of crop (with thick or thin stalks, tender or fibrous, tall or short, green or dry, etc); the characteristics of the scyther (young or old, strong or weak, small or large, etc); and the duration of the scything to be done. These small differences are due also to the fact that the scythe's process of design took its course throughout different periods, countries and continents (where local traditions, typical of peasant culture, should also be borne in mind). Nevertheless these different specific needs, traditional factors and working conditions ultimately combine to produce the same archetypal result of high formal quality.

Thus constant refinement and revision in an arc of 5,000 years have caused the design to become standard. And I dare say this ought to be the goal of every design project today, if it were only possible to shake off the hebephrenia of "new" for the sake of "new".

In the industrialized countries the scythe has a relatively marginal use. Nevertheless the peasants of the third world still live in the same conditions from which the necessity for that design first arose. In Europe its manufacture is sharply concentrated in a small number of places. I was able to visit one of these, perhaps the largest, at Dronero, in Piedmont. Production, though industrial (i.e. parcelled), retains strong elements of artisan wisdom. The starting point is always a metal bar which is heated and then gradually sharpened, curved and shaped with blows of the hammer. The work is completely manual and formation is done by eye, without the use of moulds or references. The scythe is cold-hardened during the final stages of manufacture by rapid hammering, the pattern of which is thought, by those who do not know, to be an ornamental motif.

The quality of our archetypal design is such that the cost of the implement is very low (despite the expense of highly skilled worker-craftsmen in an industrialized country). The bulk of production can thus be sold at a price accessible to third world peasant farmers. I am convinced that low cost is a sure parameter for design quality, if only because it obliges the designer to reject all the stupidities that might come into his head. The consequent form is then shaped by necessity.

Remember one last thing: in the design of a scythe no symbolic functions are involved. This also applies at times to the designing of weapons, for example, the Samurai's sword. The needs are still concerned with life and death. But in war, life and death are also part of a ritual; so that often the designing of a weapon is affected by the fact, and is permeated by its symbolic function. Try comparing the formal quality of the halberd with that of the Samurai's sword! So it can be asserted that symbolic superimposition tends to diminish formal quality (the question remains open for artefacts made for exclusively symbolic reasons). I conclude with a clarification: I am not dreaming of a mythic primitivism (agriculture today can only be mechanized). The design of a scythe can be taken as the model for the design of our living. Please don't retort with the usual sociological platitudes about our affluent society: I know them, and I say it should be changed. Is that talking like the village idiot? So what?

FERNANDO MEDINA

Spain / USA

Design, a global vision

a!, No. 14, Mexico, 1994

Although the concept of design, as we know it today, is relatively recent, its origin dates back to the beginning of mankind, having fulfilled functions similar to those of now. The evolutionary path of design is intrinsically linked to the very evolution of human beings, pushed along by their desire to make a more liveable, communicative and comfortable world.

Design begins to take a wider dimension after the Second World War, during which it was seen by industry as a necessity. This is when the industrial and technical revolutions begin to use designers, projecting design beyond its own borders.

The designer begins then to recognize that he is a professional who manages concepts, codes and aesthetics, and that his messages should be structured, programmed in a direct, clear manner, without complicated solutions in order to be easily understood and absorbed by the intended audiences. This begins to mark the difference between art and functional design.

Upon seeing that his ideas could be transmitted rapidly or instantaneously to any part of the world, thanks to the great variety of electronic means available, the designer begins acquiring a vision, increasingly global, of his role and of his planet.

Symbol to encourage peace in the world

Designers, whatever their culture or country of origin, are, in this way, tending to identify more and more with a global professional collectivity, by circulating among themselves a prolific mass of information, producing a language that supersedes their own languages. Now, taking a jump towards the future, I would take the risk of saying that designers of this future must be capable of measuring, balancing and composing concepts in their world with a planetary utility, towards a common good, without limiting themselves just to their country or society. They must be able to invent and discover solutions beyond stereotyped and hackneyed trends. Designers will be people with an advanced vision, responsible for the world they live in. They will be knowledgeable about a science that will give them the wisdom to correct and evolve, on an ongoing basis, that which becomes ineffective, proposing solutions for progress. Designers will know how to manage the

146

energy and influence that forms and colours have, taking advantage of their know-how in order to utilize it as experts in their own science. They will have overcome their tendency towards ephemeral and superficial aesthetics, taking on and integrating their true responsibilities as designers. Also, they will have developed their sense of perception, the sensitive faculty of universal language.

The time has already arrived for us to begin projecting ourselves into a present that prepares this future.

The invasion of computers, which has become so controversial, should not engender in designers any agitation, rejection or fascination. We must regard them as merely a medium that helps us evolve "our" concepts with greater speed, and variety of resources.

Designers, therefore, should not fall into the temptation of believing that computers do the thinking in design, replacing their own mechanisms of creative searching: nobody, and nothing, will take the place of that. We must simply ensure that the influence of technology doesn't neutralize or nullify the use of our own criteria in the investigation of conceptual solutions, taking advantage of their attractive and versatile facilities.

Designers, as thinking beings, must always have mental control over the technology that they utilize, since it has been thought out and created by them in order to facilitate their work and save their time.

Design is a concept that is everywhere in life itself since everything has been, is, and will be designed.

TV or not to be:
image for T-shirt

KAZUMASA NAGAI

Japan

Graphic design in Japan

Japanese graphic design is now at its peak. This is largely due to the fact that in order to win the increasingly fierce competition in public affairs and advertising among industries, an ever higher quality in design is required. It is said that about 10,000 students qualify from the design departments of universities and from art colleges every year, in the hope of becoming professional designers. This situation appears to be unique in the world. It is unlikely that they will all succeed in becoming professionals. There are already so many designers in Japan that even the media cannot employ them all.

The quality of graphic design in Japan has been elevated by this intense competition. However, it is not only the economic and social factors which determine present standards; there are also the deep roots of Japanese tradition. Foreigners often comment that graphic design from Japan, a poster for example, is very beautiful artistically, but that it fails to get across any message. AM Cassandre said "A poster is a visual telegram." Those words express the real objective of a poster – to summarize the contents and communicate them immediately, as a telegram does. Japanese posters follow the same principle, but give a different impression. That is because Japan is one of the few nations which has, with a few exceptions, only one race of people. The high standard of education has resulted in a very low rate of illiteracy and there are no great differences in the lifestyle of the people. As a result, the Japanese have an understanding which does not require words

The traditional art of Japan is both decorative and symbolic. Historically, there are very few things which can be traced back to origins in Japan. In art, for example, religious paintings, landscapes and pictures of wildlife came from China, but they were refined in Japan with new degrees of sophistication and beauty.

This sensitivity to works of art can also be seen in other, more modern areas, electronics products for example, or cars. We cannot lay claim to the original idea, but it is we who have put such subtle care into the finished product to create such high quality.

If you look at art during the period from Azuchi Momoyama to the Edo Era, the time which crystallized Japanese standards of

148

artistic beauty, you can discover elements of design even then. The door-screen painting and murals of Eitoku Kano and others, the Rin school from Sotatsu Tawaraya to Korin Ogata and Hoitsu Sakai, the woodblock prints of Utamaro Kitagawa, Hokusai Katsushika and Sharaku Toshusai, all glow with the decorative and sophisticated beauty that is uniquely Japanese.

The door-screen paintings of the Kano school, Tohaku Hasegawa and others, found in temples and castles, were executed with their role in the overall design and architecture in mind. Korin's work ranges from door-screen painting to such everyday objects as fans, boxes for stationery and calligraphy materials, pottery and even sweetmeats. The Ukiyo-e woodblock prints, which influenced some of the Impressionists such as Van Gogh and Monet, were actually portraits of some of the actors and famous beauties of the time and fulfilled the same function as photographs and posters of idols of today.

The element of design in Japanese art is an integral part of the whole. This sharp sensitivity to design is common to all Japanese and in the Edo Era it penetrated the everyday life of the ordinary people. Even artisans, living in humble rows of housing, introduced artistic harmony to their lives, their clothing and the tools they used, decorating their houses with woodblock prints.

During the Meiji Era, however, the so-called flowering of Japanese civilization, models from the west began to be hastily copied and adopted with no consideration for traditional art, crafts and design. Japan's modern graphic design was based on the posters of Cassandre and the Bauhaus, and later on American advertising and editorial design. But before long, Japanese designers began to recognize their traditional art and its decorative and symbolic value and so developed a different style of graphic design, which cannot be equalled anywhere in the world.

Japanese designers do not merely follow tradition, but understand and digest it, break it down and restructure it in a modern sense. They do not follow one single and identifiably Japanese pattern. Rather, they are full of all the variety one country and its tough competitive atmosphere can produce. The high level of printing technology, including computer plate-making, has also made a much greater variety of expression possible.

149

GÉRARD PARIS-CLAVEL

France

There is an urgent need to take one's time

gérard Paris-Clavel, since 1943. Little old man of the Alliance Graphique Internationale, free of advertising ties. Founder member of Grapus and the fresh art grocery: DO NOT BEND. Father and citizen – looking for serious professional relationships – Utopia wanted, more if we get on – free quote.

In my beautiful French country, journalists, writers and critics are not interested in posters, in images independent of the art market. There is no scientific criticism of signs and that is a great pity, for the dramatised images of life as spectacle invade us, devour us, direct us, try to change us into turds.

It is vital for these seductive-looking assailants to be resisted so that other ideas show through and can be seen.

Today's graphic art is seldom generous, creative, dealing with themes rich in humanity but instead is often out to solicit, most of the time in the service of big and small business, of the warring powers who "target" consumers to get rid of their goods as fast as possible; in other words, culture changed into a product. The brave little posters that make some sense are replaced or hidden by the vast 4 x 3 metre profit-makers.

The poster artist hardly exists nowadays; now he is a graphic artist, photographer, painter or illustrator and the poster constitutes only a small part of his output. Economic and democratic conditions make it very difficult to do high quality work. The poster often becomes part of a communications process in which it serves as an aide-memoire, a reminder of the rich, obsessive images of the press and television. Symbols are becoming symptoms – images of a consumer culture which no longer leaves us any choice.

Now, it is the choices we make that direct our lives and that is what makes people free. We are currently being released from the pain of choosing to BE and this choice, whether in politics or love, is always difficult because it is a responsibility. We are being freed of this burden in the name of HAVING, with its standard pattern clothes and standard pattern relationships. We are always being brought back to merchandise and we finish up by formulating a very simple equation: happiness equals buying, happiness equals money!

For the men of politics tied to ideologies and market interests,

VILLE MA est un MONDE

MY CITY IS A WORLD AND OUR
LIVES MIX THERE
since 1993
"I wish to express with these
words, around a 'point of view',
the idea that a city has its
neighbour cities, its suburbs,
just like countries and continents.
It's only a matter of size. I like to
think of each city as a different
part of the world, and challenge
the spectators to express their
own idea of this image. Urban
space must become again a place
for sharing, for meeting people
and for exchange, and
no longer only a place for the
circulation of things and objects.
The whole world is contained in
each city, in each neighbourhood,
just as each human being
represents the others."

URGENT: UNEMPLOYMENT
since 1992
".... It was not so long ago that
horror rose up where the unions
were no longer united, where the
workers preferred their microscopic
divisions to the great fight against
the true adversaries, which is also
necessary. So a new darkness is
born, a new fog into which the
republican device is swallowed.
It was not so long ago that
democracies died for not knowing
how and not wanting to make all
men equal and for disdaining
brotherhood."
Jean-Pierre Grunfeld

this way of operating is the only solution and their demagogy has
to be sold like an amnesiac product. The future of politics is ever
more linked to the standards inflicted by the merchants; they are
not ashamed to take advantage of everything, to put an ecological
or humanist endorsement on their goods. Faced with their ads, one
can only deplore the absence of high quality humanist expression
representing forces of progress.

It is sad to see the vast bulk of public, cultural and humanitarian
associations and institutions falling into line with these criteria. They
are fascinated by the media of advertising which appears to provide a
means to an end which they think they can bring under their own
control. They play the game for fear of being left out of it. They are
encouraged in this by the advertising agencies who tout for business,
trying to get their hands on more and more such themes "of public
benefit" that can be converted into "markets", all with the help of
crisis and competition. The associations and institutions keep on
raising the stakes, powerfully backed by logos. The sign takes over
from the crown or the signet ring, it becomes the coat-of-arms and
the shield of the prince who has turned into a frog-manager or frog-
MD to await a kiss from the public that never comes.

Only the business frogs are in their right, logical place splashing
in the profit pond. The others should not, ought not, be there.

It cuts ordinary citizens out of the dialogue; any public expression
of popular feeling is stifled by the aesthetic concerns of us the
professionals. Let us wake up to the contact we have lost and work
from close-to on reforging our acquaintance with everyday issues.
As the writer john Berger declared, "Our sole duty at the moment
is to listen to those who cannot be heard."

Faced with mass poverty, we do not have the right to wait! The
distress of the excluded stares us in the face day after day.

It seems that for the government technocrats, the power-holding
elites don't have the same waiting conditions as us. In their world
there is security of employment without genuine, close contact
with the people it is their duty to represent and defend. But for
them, talking takes over from dialogue, image takes over from a
programme and it's bye-bye to trust!

Their projects, constantly on hold, always have no effect
whatsoever on everyday life. Yet social inequalities and the lies
of the media are going beyond the bounds of decency.

When can we express our individuality on a question in some
cultural way? Place our subjectivity in tension with the collective
mind? Bring out conflicts between citizens. Where and how can
a genuine cultural policy express itself? There are too few terrains
available for applied experiments, and none at all for research. Yet
think what is at stake; whether we like it or not, expression is the
means of conveyance of our ideas.

The lonely work of the individual *auteur* committed to quality

151

and the meaningfulness of his work within a nurturing collective environment is vital; complementary interprofessional relationships and mutual exchange in our ways of creating bring with them new ways of relating and producing. New associative networks have to be found to break down the isolation of "specialists", to better withstand the economic pressure imposed by the latest order received. This will encourage artists to play a larger role in shared activities, will hold in check their tendency to become isolated, to want cultural comfort, to confuse individualism and freedom in the creative process, to confuse cocktails and petit fours and the social struggle.

What interest me are subjects that ask questions. And of course the utopia of an egalitarian society. That is what makes sense of my work with forms; forms in themselves have no power, it is what they contain of the real world which expresses ugliness or beauty. Art is necessarily politically non-conformist! Thinking like that at the present time is not good for getting work, it marginalises you. This is not fair, for graphic art, by operating in this way, contributes to the critical training of those who look at it by adding curiosity and doubts to their reflection on the message. Because it awakens a desire to swap opinions and not to hold your tongue and give in to the ready-made responses of merchandising.

At a time when we are being drowned in visual and televisual diarrhoea, when advertising's capitalist realism and its media motorways are providing an answer for everything, the artistic practice of image-making graphic artists can make questions be asked!

I'm thoroughly convinced that, alongside the search for good design, there is one goal that naturally takes priority; working together for human causes. To me, one thing is fundamental in this world we all share: there is an urgent need to take one's time.

Gérard Paris-Clavel – 1994

Recycled environment-friendly text consisting of 40% fresh grey matter and 60% extracts from various debates organised with the DO NOT BEND association

For further information and current address:

After Grapus's extinction, after Cocolux was put to sleep, and after I left Graphistes Associés in June 1992, I am currently working, when I please, as a freelance and with the DO NOT BEND association

at: 11 place Voltaire – 94200 Ivry sur Seine – France

MICHAEL PETERS

UK

Europe can cash in

Marketing, London, 16 June 1994

In Italy last month I spied a poster of a semi-naked woman on horseback who gazed coyly at me from beneath her lashes. This apparently was Europa riding to greater European glory, but the less astute might have been forgiven for thinking she was Lady Godiva or La Cicciolina.

Existing European imagery is poor: media-buffeted voters went to the polls last week seeing stars and little else. But if, in 1999, we achieve economic unity, European citizens will have a tangible piece of Community design rattling around in their pockets.

The most important determinant of such a design will be the balance of power in Brussels: if Europe evolves into a federal superstate, the currency will symbolize its authority; if it exists to protect autonomous nation states, the tender will combine national and European imagery.

Eventually, money will emerge into a single card, charged up at banking points and swiped through a subtracter when purchasing. But in 1999, traditional tender will be issued. Possibly paper and metal alloy will give way to colourful slivers of plastic, but these lack substance in handling. It is high time, however, that braille dots distinguished the denominations for visually impaired people.

Symbols of European unity for our currency are few and far between: Europa and the stars are outdated; the featureless uniformity of the Palais de l'Europe or the European Monetary Institute would cause devaluation in protest; and an image of Community achievement, such as the Ariane rocket, conjures up images of Soviet propaganda. I prefer the abstract: atoms orbiting around electrons are almost magical, mystical in their unity; most bizarrely, a unicorn – a horse designed by committee – a mythical beast at one with itself.

Traditionally, national currencies have confined their imagery to prosaic heads of state and historical figures – such things are *verboten* on our fiscal unit. Let's read lines of poetry and prose (better than Berlitz) or take solace in art. Adulthood does not dictate that we put childish things away: the French have incorporated drawings from Saint-Exupéry's *Little Prince* on their fifty-franc note; this should serve as an inspiration for Belgians to brandish Tintin and

153

the Bank of England to seek refuge behind Paddington Bear.

National games, foods, or architectural projects like the Tower of Pisa restoration and the bridge over the Sound between Sweden and Denmark would provide themed snippets of information for the consumer to compare. Notes could become advertisements to titillate the traveller, as figures in local dress cavort against a scenic backdrop swinging shopping bags from famous arcades.

This currency will be one of the most powerful communication tools in the world and as such it should surely incorporate some educational content. On one side of the tender, let's learn to count from one to ten in the languages of Europe, say please and thank you and ask for a beer. On the reverse, national maps will be printed which fit together across denominations to produce a geographical jigsaw of Europe, display international time zones, the constellations in the sky at night, and best of all, the weather. After all, the Brits must have something to talk about.

TULLIO PERICOLI

Italy

The king's table

The King's Table, Munich, Germany, 1993

T he king is His Majesty. He has a kingdom of his own, a territory over which he exercises his power. He isn't privileged. Indeed, he is just like many other people. There is something of a king in all of us. Maybe we are kings of small things, tiny territories composed of very few subjects. It might be that we establish a sovereign power or an iron dictatorship over a limited area of our own home.

Even the artist is a king. He rules over a minute kingdom whose borders are well defined: the table. At first, he lays down the borders in such a way as to ensure their freedom from invasion. And the edges – the limits of his territory – may be rendered eventful by impassable forests, tangled vegetation and white, lifeless spaces which nobody would dare to venture beyond. Here, the artist judges and rules supreme. He knows that within his hands he holds the sweet, seductive world of codes and laws whose very order and issue depend upon him. His commands, issued in accordance with the law, will organize the lives of persons and things in his kingdom. They will even regulate the gait, steps and material movements within the territory, and establish the hierarchies between things and people, and between people and places.

Rigid law enforcement is not, however, a regal habit. Like all other kings, the artist is inconsistent and contradictory. His power becomes will, childlike caprice. He loves to propose laws only so as to contradict and overturn them. He doesn't wish to seem predictable. He sets traps for his subjects in order that he might surprise them and observe their sudden bewilderment. In reality, this is the time set aside for fun, games and recreation. This is the moment when solitude can be overcome. Just like a game, the imagination of the king comes into action to confront that of his subjects. On the table, pens, paper and colours come alive. Forests, haunted places, unknown beauties, horsemen, animals and hunts appear. A magical repertoire of people and objects swarm about and spill over into the kingdom. Emerging out of nowhere, they hide and they wriggle away. They seem to be fixed but are only propped up, as if they were about to fly away suddenly.

And the king, who had apparently been amused while pursuing

them, looks on as they resist, get organized, and carry out their independent decision to become real themselves – more real than the king himself. The territory has its own rules which are more powerful than any others which might be agreed upon for a game. This is the time when the king himself feels overpowered: merely another playing card in a pack of fifty-two. On the table, written in colour, his biography and his destiny. King and kingdom, bound by the same omens, are exactly the same thing: both false, or both really true.

JOSEP PLA-NARBONA

Spain

omments about art and graphics

Art and Graphics, eds Willy Rotzler and Jacques N. Garamond,
Zurich, ABC Verlag, 1983

W e tend to assume that people who enter the life of the Arts must possess creative sensibility. It is therefore clear that contemporary art exercises a direct influence on such people as soon as they concern themselves with the pictorial adaptation of an idea.

I have come to this understanding after thirty years of activity in the field of applied art. Having also been active in graphic design, which is also one of the applied arts, I have always kept the practical aspect in view, since this is a component of every form of advertising. I have always been concerned with the "philosophy" of a message that has to be generally communicated.

If we follow Hegel in defining philosophy as "the thinking contemplation of the self-unfolding of reason," my approach as a graphic artist has been first analytical, then logical, and finally critical, speculative and aesthetic. My point of departure is a system, within which I ascertain a truth and then represent it pictorially; for in the final analysis, every commercial train of thought has its own justification and its appropriate pictorial expression.

Full freedom in artistic creation seems to me to be the basis of all contemporary art: but freedom is a concept which very often does not coincide with the practical demands of today's advertising and marketing. Applied graphics, on the other hand, is a service, and it would be pretentious to believe that through commercial art a wider public can be made aware of the problematic of free art.

This leads to the assumption that the expression of freedom, which underlies every genuine work of art, comes from reflection on man and his environment. If I may express it philosophically: an anthropological vision. By anthropology I mean the science of man as a psycho-physical individual. Anthropology proceeds from the perception of man as a biological being, but at the same time it apprehends the psychic side of his nature, which is closely linked with his socio-cultural environment. In short: only the artist who is really gifted and possesses this "anthropological" vision can influence a wider public over and above the advertising message, by holding fast to the substance of his personal system of values. And this, in the final analysis, is that which constitutes genuine art.

Información y sociedad actual

Book cover

157

PAULA SCHER

USA

The devaluation of design by the design community

AIGA Journal, **New York, 1994**

What's wrong with this picture?

The Cooper-Hewett Museum selected five designers in a paid competition (base price $1,000, though some reportedly got more) to create a new identity for the museum. The winner was then awarded the job.

ID magazine considered a number of designers for its redesign and asked at least one of them to provide comps on spec, but did not award him the job.

The Industrial Designers Society of America (IDSA) contacted three or more design firms requesting a "proposal" for their new identity package even though it was a pro bono job, because they didn't want to show favoritism. They received some critical responses from some of the design groups they approached, rescinded their policy, and awarded one firm the unpaid job.

The AIGA, which had assigned their annual jacket to a designer on a pro bono basis plus $1,000 to cover expenses, decided that the jacket was too important a marketing tool to rely on what the designated designer submitted. The institute changed its policy and requested a minimum of three sketches from the chosen designer, while the assignment remained pro bono and the expense money remained $1,000.

The previous events occurred in the last year and a half. In that same time period, MTV, a winner of the AIGA Design Leadership Award, asked twenty designers and illustrators to create political art for the cause of their choice, to be aired at the MTV Music Video Awards ceremony and to be printed in the program. The artists were requested to produce this art for a fee of $500, which would be donated to any charity they designated, with MTV matching the donation. (MTV is owned by Viacom, which is currently locked in the Paramount takeover battle.)

Each organization operated with apparently altruistic motives inspired by the design communities they support. In three cases, the organizations are not-for-profit and rely on funds given by the communities they support. They are aware that many designers would love to work on their projects for prestige or exposure or the opportunity to produce award-winning graphics, and they emphasize this as the selling point for the free work. In fact, with so many designers available and eager to work for so little, they probably feel the need to be fair about it and spread the opportunity around. When one considers this line of thinking, it's not surprising that MTV would follow in kind with the added kicker of political-cause affiliation. And suddenly Seagram's has developed a similar attitude toward its annual report, which it touts as "a marvellous opportunity for exposure with cachet for any good designer." They asked three firms to compete and produce several ideas on spec.

These events can be blamed on the economy or on the overpopulation of the design community, or, when one gets really farfetched, on young designers using computers. If one is employed by an educational or other institution, a corporation, a publication, or an organization that supports, promotes, or is allied with graphic design in some way but does not rely on a paying clientele other than designers for survival, one can ignore these events altogether and assume they speak only to the commercially competitive concerns of design firms.

Unfortunately, they speak to all of us. They are the symptom of a design community contemptuous of itself, a community so splintered by social, political, academic, sexual, regional and aesthetic factionalism that it has lost sight of its original collective goals.

When I first became active in the AIGA in the 1970s, its goals were very clear: to promote, protect and document the profession of graphic design and to encourage, support and recognize quality work. What made the AIGA especially appealing was its stated tenet: the AIGA was about design, not designers. The belief was that by elevating the profession of graphic design, the AIGA would also elevate design value to the American business and civic communities and thereby improve the visual standards and expectations of our society. The notion of value here had very little to do with money. Money is only one American symbol of value. The AIGA was interested in the power of the design progression, the ability of good graphic designers to become powerful enough individually and collectively to persuade cumbersome bureaucracies that good design is good business and good for society.

How to do it? Organize a national community of designers. Publish. Involve the educational community. Alert the press. Create a journal, develop dialogue and criticism. Record history. Stage a national conference. Create professional practice guidelines. Encourage press coverage. Create awareness.

The events and activities of the design community in the 1980s and 1990s remind me of almost every boxing movie I've ever seen. The young idealistic fighter who has trained hard, has good family values, and a nice girl back home, hooks up with a ne'er do well promoter with mob ties, who quickly pushes the young boxer to fame and fortune so heady and corrupt that our hero forgets his early family values one by one. He dumps the girl back home, compromises his principles, breaks his immigrant father's heart, and finally breaks his fingers so he can neither fight nor play the violin. Moral of the story: don't forget your values.

In the 1980s the design community witnessed the great rise of "professionalism" (now a euphemism for the production of non-innovative but stylishly acceptable work, usually in corporate communications, coupled with very good fees). Along with "professionalism" came the "business consultant to the designers," who proclaimed, "Design is a business".

This became the mantra of the 1980s. The AIGA, along with other organizations and publications, produced seminars, conferences, and special magazine issues devoted to the business of design. They were followed by a plethora of design self-help books, which told you how to set up your own business, how to promote, how to speak correct business jargon, how to dress, how to buy insurance, and so on.

There was nothing inherently wrong with this except for the subsequent confusion it caused. "Professional" work looked more professional, and corporate communications in general were visually improved. The level of design mediocrity rose. Also, practising designers as a rule had previously been rather sloppy about running their businesses. They were easily taken advantage of, didn't know how to construct proposals, and were generally more interested in designing than in minding the store, networking, or planning for the future. The business seminars did no harm, but the political and economic climate of the 1980s in general, coupled with the pervasiveness of the "Design is a business" hype, perverted the design community's overall goal. The goal became money.

HOW and *Step-by-Step Graphics* magazines were born in this climate. Both publications explained how to be a professional graphic designer. A young reader could learn how to set up a design business, how to furnish it, how to buy equipment, how to make a design and sell it to a client, and how to do award-winning work just as the rich and famous designers featured in the magazine did.

It was not surprising that enrolments at colleges with halfway decent design programs shot up in the 1980s. Graphic design had become a viable profession with the promise of glamor and success. In the 1950s and 1960s, graphic design had been a relatively obscure profession, largely undocumented and poorly reported. As a profession it seemed risky, populated with talented mavericks and not a place where a person could count on making a living. The 1980s' publications changed all that. If the goal of the AIGA was to change the general perception of graphic design and create awareness of the profession, then this was our greatest area of success – an ambiguous success at best.

With all the young designers graduating from various design programs and entering the field, the design publishing boom was on. More and more awards competitions were founded, more magazines, more books on type, trends, letterhead design, package design, shopping-bag design, trademark design, magazine design, the history of design, famous designers, famous designers from California, famous designers under forty, women designers, alternative design books featuring people left out of other books, and books one could buy into to use for self-promotion.

The proliferation of graphic design books in the 1980s and 1990s made all trends readily apparent and ripe for immediate imitation. The graphics publications began reporting on design trends like fashion columnists watching hemlines. Trends were news. Even the general press could understand them. Recently an article in *The New York Times* "Style" section reported how the typeface Bodoni has become a popular style in magazine design. I never saw the word "Bodoni" in *The New York Times* before, but I don't think this is what we had in mind when we wanted to create general graphic design awareness.

The increased number of annual award shows put a new financial and professional burden on the design community, a heightened sense of obligation to promote, be noticed, published, acclaimed, and have a national presence in every annual, in all compendiums now appearing, in total, almost monthly. The pressure was considerably less on older designers with established reputations and recognizable work. For unknown young designers working on corporate communications, promotional material, obscure packaging, and obscure magazines, being noticed was more and more impossible. The last design firm to gain a national standing through design annuals was The Duffy Design Group, in the mid-1980s. If there is no substantial change in the number of annuals and frequency of publication, no designer or design group will gain that kind of national prominence again. The mass of work displayed in the total annual publishing output cancels out new designers. Familiar names remain familiar and unfamiliar names stay unfamiliar.

Pick up a *Communication Arts Design Annual* and thumb through it, then flip through *Print's Regional Design Annual*. Follow it up with an *AIGA Annual*, then breeze through the graphic design section of the *New York Art Directors Club Annual, Graphis Design*, The American Center for Design 100 Show, the *ID Annual Review*, and wind it all up with the *Type Directors Club Annual*. Do it all in one sitting and don't read any of the copy. Make sure they are all from the same year, or at most a year or two apart. The effect will be a numbing sameness. There are some general stylistic differences in the work selected by various annuals, but only when one confronts the same piece three or four times in different books does that individual piece develop a character of its own, separate from the rest of the work in the publication. In fact, one could generalize about contemporary graphic design as viewed in annuals exactly the way Paul Rand did in his essay "From Cassandre to Chaos" in *Design: Form and Chaos*. Rand's "analysis" of stylistic approaches is separated from the intent and content of the work. It overgeneralizes the way annuals do.

Several years ago I thumbed through an *Art Directors Club Annual* from the mid-fifties. The print ads all seemed to have dumb line-drawings of creatures with smiley faces that closely resembled the drawings in Paul Rand's El Producto ads. The drawings were coupled with quaint, poorly letter-spaced typography, some of it stencilled, some of it, apparently, in alternating colors (the annual was black-and-white), and some of it with cute little curlicues at the ends of the letter forms. The El Producto ads may have been in there too; I honestly don't recall. I just remember that everything looked the same – all style and no substance.

Design annuals, as most of them are constructed, trivialize work. More design annuals trivialize work more. To view work critically, one needs time for reflection and perspective. When we trivialize our work we trivialize our profession. Voluminous publishing without careful analysis and reflection does more harm than good. It was not surprising that by the end of the "Design is business"-ridden 1980s, we got good and disgusted with our own rhetoric. The "Dangerous Ideas" AIGA National Conference in San Antonio in 1989, which attempted to highlight important social issues, was a refreshing change from the 1987 conference in San Francisco, which highlighted an insurance salesman. I applaud two social themes explored at the conferences: that wasteful packaging is a pollutant and we need to take responsibility for it; and that our communications can be powerful and damaging to people, so we need to take responsibility for them.

Actually, the messages are the same. We are responsible for our work and its consequences. Responsibility is a crucial part of our professional ethic. We are also responsible (according to our original goals) for encouraging and supporting quality design, therefore, racism, sexism, and other forms of personal prejudice have no place in the design community.

That said, I believe that the phrase "social relevance" has replaced "Design is a business" as a mantra for the 1990s. Confusing social issues with design issues is dangerous. They're not the same.

It's hard to write this with dispassion because I hate mass mantras. I never trust or believe them because they always pervert themselves, even when the mantra is in sync with my own views. Progressive political and social beliefs are generally life-long, deeply held convictions, not transient group mores. Yes, consciousness can be raised, and I always love it when someone who voted for Ronald Reagan wakes up and smells the coffee, but I'm nervous when we try to make converts through the AIGA or *ID* magazine. If they're that easily converted they may respond just as positively to the mantra of the next decade, which could well turn out to be fascism.

The "social relevance" mantra disturbs me mostly because it confuses and diminishes our primary goals. It becomes easy to decry graphic design as a trivial profession. If one factors in all the world wars, diseases, poverty, illiteracy and natural disasters, a well-designed hang-tag is silly. But I don't think the responsibility for the visual environment of our society is silly or trivial, and collectively, that is our charge.

"Social relevance" can also become a stranger criterion for judging design. I was on a jury last year with a judge who voted for work on the basis of the organization that commissioned the work. This is okay if the point of the exhibition is to highlight politically correct organizations. But if the point is design excellence, a poorly designed brochure for an AIDS benefit is not better than a brilliantly designed brochure for an investment banking company, no matter how much one's sympathies run toward the AIDS brochure.

The recently created Chrysler Awards for innovation in design offer a cash prize of $10,000 to architects, product designers and graphic designers for their individual contributions to society. The items in their definition of design excellence for graphic design appeared in this order: 1. Sustainability (environmentally sensitive) 2. Accessibility (seen by people) 3. Technology (the appropriate use of) 4. Communication (successfully speaks to its audience) 5. Beauty (that extra aesthetic "something" that sets the design apart).

Had we been constantly reinforcing our original goals, the first three parts of this definition would be irrelevant, merely an expected aspect of any responsible design. But here, "communication" and "beauty" are last, implying that the design community is so irresponsible it cannot meet the minimum requirements. An environmentally sensitive design that doesn't communicate is a real waste of paper – even unbleached, recycled paper with the proper amount of post-consumer waste. Environmentally sensitive design that actually communicates its message but looks like such holy hell that you don't want it in your home, on your desk, or in your hands for one minute is still a piece of garbage. Visual environmentalism matters, now more than ever.

Overall design goals also become confused when they are coupled with "women's issues". Women represent the largest percentage of the design community holding the lowest-paying jobs. They feel robbed of opportunity, prestige, and even history. They are constantly confronted with the previous and still powerful generation of male design leaders, who, through their generational culture, remain inherently sexist and completely unaware of their bad behavior. There's valid reason for anger.

163

Also, women as a group face a real struggle in overcoming centuries of sociological baggage. They must confront their own fears of self assertion, management and success. Here, the Special Interest Groups provided by AIGA on the chapter level are immensely helpful and successful.

But there is a tremendous danger of enforcing women's issues at the expense of the design community's primary goals. Blatant tokenism implies that a standard is being breached. Contemporary women's shows and books also have the same implication. They inadvertently set different criteria for judging the work of women and may serve to diminish real achievement, not promote it.

At the AIGA Conference in Miami, some women were infuriated by the small number of women invited to speak. (Five women were asked – one cancelled – while twenty men participated as speakers.) The number is low when we consider how many terrific women practitioners, educators and writers with something important to contribute there are. But what was worse was that three of the speakers were giving talks that had the word "women" in the title. This implied that women speak only on women's issues. In the planning of this conference, women had accidentally become segregated, operating under a separate agenda. Their anger was focused on the number of women, not the content of the speeches.

I'm sure that the conference organizers meant well. Here, women's issues were addressed in three presentations, more than any other single issue. However, this kind of thinking, either by or for women, is ultimately more damaging to women and the design community than it is helpful. Women's issues and overall design goals don't necessarily reinforce one another and they may create destructive factionalism.

But an even broader example of angry factionalism that damages our community is something I have to call "ageism", simply for want of a better word. "Ageism" reflects the divide between what is perceived to be East Coast "Establishment" designers, largely from an older generation, and younger designers with differing cultural and aesthetic sensibilities. Some ageism can be defined as "regionalism" because a lot of the aesthetic splits have to do with technologically experimental design emanating from the West Coast. Some ageism returns to "women's issues" when it involves splits between the so-called East Coast Establishment and women who head aesthetic movements (like Kathy McCoy at Cranbrook or Lorraine Wilde at Cal Arts), or socially oriented design movements (like Sheila de Bretteville at Yale). Or ageism can be perceived as the split between establishment/practising designers and academic/experimental designers.

Aesthetic debate is crucial to our community and has always existed. The modernism/eclecticism debate has raged for years while devout practitioners on both sides have come together in mutual admiration and respect because their goal is always the same: quality in graphic design for the betterment of business and society.

With ageism, fear, loathing and disrespect bury our overall design goal. The goal of ageism is power, but not the power and influence of the design community as a whole. It becomes a power struggle within the various political and aesthetic factions to win control of the debate to define quality. As I've stated previously, I'm wary about value being defined by social and political agendas. But the aesthetic debate has become unnecessarily ugly, divisive and destructive.

I'm not sure how ageism came to be. Its roots start in the early 1980s with the tremendous growth of the design industry and the pervasion of its original goals. With the increase of design publishing and the proliferation of annuals, the older generation of designers became distanced from the younger generation. They stopped learning their names. (I think the last generation absorbed included Woody Pirtle and Michael Vanderbyl.) When they stopped learning young designers' names, the veterans of graphic design began to refer to the work in terms of stylistic elements like "layering", "letter spacing", "leading", "retro", and finally, "that computer stuff". That there was appropriate and inappropriate use of each element became lost on them, simply because of the pervasiveness of it all. (Exactly my response when I looked at that 1950s *Art Directors Club Annual*.) The work had become all style and no substance.

Knowing (and liking) an individual helps to mute competitive animosities caused by distinct aesthetic differences. In the New York design community, Pushpin and Herb Lubalin lived harmoniously with Vignelli and Rudy deHarak. They all knew one another. Theoretically speaking Massimo Vignelli should be as repulsed by Ed Benguiat's work as he is by that of Rudy Vanderlans. But Massimo knows Ed. Ed is a fine fellow, and after all, they both agree that what matters most is the continual striving for quality. Their goals are the same even if they approach them from different directions.

But the young designers featured in annuals and articles have become faceless and therefore valueless to this Eastern Establishment. For at least the past five years, Henry Wolf has opened every speech with "Back in the days when design was design..." The unspoken end of the phrase is "... as opposed to today when everything stinks." This implication is not lost on its audience, and over time it builds a certain resentment.

A progressive community turns reactionary when it believes it is about to lose something. This couldn't be more true of the Eastern Establishment. New technology has totally revolutionized the method, craft and structure of design practices that have existed for forty years. The technological shift has been coupled with a devastated

165

economy, particularly on the East Coast. In the midst of layoffs, price reductions and a general sense of demoralization, healthy perspectives become elusive. The computer is seen as an evil enemy, a dangerous tool in the hands of valueless incompetents bent on destroying the design profession. When this fear is coupled with strange social agendas by some design groups, angry women, and bizarre experimental work by design schools receiving an amazing amount of press attention, suddenly it looks like the whole world is going to the dogs. The standards of quality are being destroyed.

The question then becomes, What is quality work? This is the eternal debate. We know design must function properly, but design functions differently for different problems and audiences. *Ray Gun* works perfectly for its audience but won't be received well by someone over forty-five who doesn't care about rock 'n' roll. Is it quality or garbage? Aesthetics is a tricky business.

One can admire the aesthetics of a specific school without loving it. I admire *Emigré* without loving it. It's ten years old now. I admire the publication and some of the typefaces even though I'll never use them. But the *Emigré* designers were innovators. I felt the same way about Herb Lubalin. In fact, I feel the same way about Paul Rand. I never loved his work as I love Cassandre's, El Lissitzky's, Pierre Mendell's and some of Fred Woodward's *Rolling Stone* spreads. But I admire it. I know how important it is. One builds admiration from a distance, in retrospect. It takes time.

With ageism there is no admiration for any work produced by a younger generation. None. No shining example, no beacon among the heathens. It's all bad: Neville Brody, bad; *Emigré*, garbage; Fabien Baron, a ripoff of Brodovitch; Chuck Anderson, too many advertising cuts; Cranbrook, feh; Rick Valicenti; PU., et cetera. And pretty soon there's nothing left to eat. Only designers from their own generation of the distant past merit praise. At the end, there is no debate, no enlightenment – only a divide. And we are all losers.

We are losers because the ensuing factionalism, hurt feelings, confusion, resentment and anger are damaging to the most important goals of the community. If we fear and loathe one another, how can we persuade society of the collective value of good design? If we're all chopped into different factions with different agendas, collectively we have no power at all. We destroy our credibility. When we are contemptuous of one another, we invite the contempt of business and society. We devalue design.

Every day I find myself in supermarkets, discount drugstores, video shops, and other environments that are obviously untouched by our community. No "bad Brody" or "*Emigré* garbage" or, for that matter, no "saintly" Vignelli, Rand or Glaser. Just plain old-fashioned non-controversial bad design, the kind of anonymous bad design we've come to ignore because we're too busy fighting over the aesthetics of the latest AIGA poster. We don't talk or write about it, it heads no one's agenda, but it's still most of America.

So I come back to my petty list at the beginning of this article. What's wrong with the pictures is that four organizations that exist in support of design demonstrated that they have absolutely no idea how to hire or work with a graphic designer. Responding to the contemptuous, factionalized climate we have created, they have pitted designers against one another in competition for free work and they have lost sight of the fact that pro bono is a donation. They assume that the designer's benefit from the free job is greater than theirs. (With all the angry criticism they receive from the various design camps regardless of what is produced, maybe they have a point.) Yet, for all our annuals, seminars, conferences, political and sexual consciousness-raising groups, environmental lectures, aesthetic manifestos and diatribes, respect and understanding of the profession of graphic design is worse than it was in the 1970s.

At the end of all the boxing movies the fighter always learns that his original ideals were valid, but things went wrong when the ideals were perverted, corrupted and abandoned. The same lesson applies to us.

NIKLAUS TROXLER

Switzerland

Personal initiative is in demand!

Lecture: Brno Design Biennale, 1994

Today, we are not only aware of an increase in ecological damage but also of an equally annoying visual environmental vandalism. It is admittedly noticeable that environmental issues are increasingly gaining in importance in the activities of the designer. This appears to be logical as the danger to our environment and thus to our elementary living conditions is taking on increasingly threatening forms. As designers, our task is to stimulate the general public to sensible behaviour. In like manner, we are also called upon to point out social injustices.

In the recent past, I have had various opportunities to achieve goals such as these.

In 1992, I was invited, with colleagues from all over the world, to design a poster for the Environmental Congress in Rio. My entry, which showed bleeding tree stumps and contained no text, was rejected by the organisers, however, as they interpreted it as an insult to Brazilian environmental policies. My aim was to offer a form of poster that was comprehensible to all. The whole world could grasp its meaning. In the end, I sent in a different entry which was then accepted.

Concerned by this decision, I decided – overcoming my own cowardice – to publish the rejected poster in Switzerland myself. I talked to my screen printer about the possibility of working together. He expressed his willingness and we shared the resulting costs. I discussed the project with the billboard company: they were also very generous. Six hundred posters were then printed and went on display all over Switzerland. There was no shortage of reactions: many newspapers reacted positively and many passers-by wrote to me in positive tones. This personal initiative of mine had proved more than worthwhile!

Last year, I started another personal initiative of my own: shocked by a TV broadcast of a reconstruction of an attack on a defenceless woman in a Zurich street – during which passers-by showed no inclination to intercede – I reacted from a deep sense of concern.

I wished to do something to combat this violence; the increase in

168

racial hatred also strengthened my motivation. I began to think about making a poster. With my draft STOP THE VIOLENCE, I spoke to my screen printer and the billboard company again. The reactions of both partners were very positive. The campaign started with a run of over 1,400 posters which went on display throughout German-speaking Switzerland. The reaction of the public and media was overwhelming. We were compelled to do a second run of the poster as many communities, church parishes, schools and neighbourhood associations had requested copies. In the end, we also printed a large number of postcards which were distributed to interested parties.

Once again: personal initiative proved to be worthwhile!

I am currently involved with a new subject for a personal initiative campaign: I would again like to address the public on the topic of "Tolerance brings Peace." Now I am sure I can rely on my screen printer and the billboard company – my partners!

Biographies of Contributors

Saul Bass
Born 1920. Died 1996. Graphic designer of numerous trademarks and corporate identity programmes. Creator of motion picture titles. Director of short films, epilogues, special sequences in feature films. Awarded Oscar for "Why Man Creates". Chairman and Creative Director of Bass Yager & Associates, New York.

Ruedi Baur
Born 1956. Created the studio intégral concept (Paris and Stuttgart) in 1989. Specialises in two-or three-dimensional identification, orientation and information programmes. Co-ordinator of the post-diploma design at the Ecole Nationale des Beaux-Arts, Lyon.

Félix Beltrán
Born in Havana, Cuba. Studied and worked in New York in the 1950s. Has written five books and many articles, and has received over 100 design awards. He has lived in Mexico since 1983.

Pierre Bernard
Born in Paris, 1942. Formed Grapus in 1970 and the Atelier de Création Graphique in 1991. Lives in Paris and teaches graphic design at the Ecole Supérieure des Arts Décoratifs.

Michael Bierut
A partner in the New York office of Pentagram.

Professor Karl Oskar Blase
Born 1925 in Cologne. After degree in graphic design, he ran his own studio. Became design consultant for the Amerika-Häuser in Germany 1952 and Professor at the Universität Kassel in 1966. Participant at document exhibitions.

Pieter Brattinga
Born 1931. Professor and chairman of the department of advertising design and visual communication at Pratt Institute 1960-63. Editor and designer of a series of experimental publications, *Quadrat Prints,* for Steendrukkerij de Jong & Co., Hilversum, 1957-74. Since 1964 has been a partner of Form Mediation International, Amsterdam, designing catalogues, posters and exhibitions for the Rijksmuseum Kroller-Muller, Otterlo. Design consultant to the Dutch State Mines.

Mimmo Castellano
For more than forty years has been trying to interest his fellow Italians in good public graphic design. With a very few exceptions in the 1960s, he feels his attempts have been useless. He is now looking for intellectual asylum.

Ken Cato
Born in Australia, 1946. Studied at the Royal Melbourne Institute of Technology and worked in a number of studios before establishing Cato Hibberd Design in 1970. The practice evolved into Cato Design, Melbourne, with offices round the Pacific Rim, specializing in packaging, corporate identity and editorial design.
Winner of many awards in the southern hemisphere, founder member and chairman (1980) of the Australian Writers and Art Directors Association.

Louis Danziger
Born 1923. Began as apprentice in the art department of a New York printer. Studied at the Los Angeles Art Center School of Design and briefly under Alexey Brodovitch at the New School for Social Research. Taught at the LA Art Centre School 1956-62 and Chouinard Art Institute 1963-72; director of graphic design at the California Institute of the Arts, Valencia 1972-88. Design consultant to among others Atlantic Richfield Company 1978-86, and for the 1984 LA Olympic Games.

Gert Dumbar

Born 1940. Studied painting and graphic design in The Hague. Founded the graphic design department of Tel Design Association, which he left in 1977 to found Studio Dumbar. The studio's clients have included Wang, Philips, IBM, the Dutch PTT, and the Rijksmuseum, and their design programmes have won many awards. Dumbar was visiting professor at the Royal College of Art 1985-87, chairman of the Dutch Association of Graphic Designers, and president of British Designers and Art Directors Association (1987-88).

Gene Federico

Born in New York,1918. Pratt Institute graduate, 1938. Art director in various advertising agencies until co-founded Lord, Geller, Federico 1967. Art Directors Club Hall of Fame Laureate 1980. American Institute of Graphic Arts medalist 1987. Honorary Doctorate, New School/ Parsons 1990. Life Achievement Award, Pratt Institute 1990. Type Directors Club Medalist 1991.

Alan Fletcher

Alan Fletcher's international design reputation is reflected by his commissions from major corporations and cultural institutions around the world. He began his career in New York in 1959, co-founded Fletcher/Forbes/Gill in 1962, was a founding partner of Pentagram in 1972, and left Pentagram to open his own studio in 1992.

Shigeo Fukuda

Born in Tokyo, 1932. Graduated from Tokyo National University of Fine Arts and Music, 1956, and joined Ajinomoto Co. Ltd. Since leaving the company in 1958 he has freelanced. Received the Gold Medal at the International Poster Biennale, Warsaw, 1972, had a one-man show at the Asian Art Museum, San Francisco in 1987 and at the Quimper Centre d'Art Contemporain in 1992. Has been inducted into the New York Art Directors Club Hall of Fame. He is Vice-President of JAGDA and a member of RDI.

Jacques Garamond

Born 1910. Graphic artist, professor of graphic art. Has created logos, trademarks and packaging. Artistic consultant to inter-national organisations: UNESCO, Marshall Plan, Air France, SNCF, CIBA Suisse. Founder of Alliance Graphique Internationale.

Christof Gassner

Born in Zurich, 1941. Studied there at the Kunstgewerbeschule. Works as a graphic designer and typographer in Darmstadt and teaches at the University of Kassel. Art director of *Öko-Test Magazin* 1985-90, and of the magazine *Natur*, 1992.

John Gorham

Worked as a designer for the *Daily Mirror* and *Sunday Mirror* publicity department, and the *Sunday Times* marketing department in the 1960s, then as an art director at Cassons Advertising Agency. Freelance since 1969.

Franco Grignani

Born near Pavia, Italy. Studied architecture but later turned to painting, experimental photography and graphic design. Believes research into the new discoveries of science and psychology to be the basis for any aesthetic experience. Planned and designed the graphic art section at the Triennale in Milan, 1965. Lives and works in Milan.

Rudolph deHarak

Began his career as a painter and designer in 1946. In addition to his design practice, has taught design at Yale University and been Professor of Design at The Cooper Union School of Art and Architecture, New York. Amongst his many awards he has received the Gold Medal from the American Institute of Graphic Arts and the Presidential Design Award (1985), and has been inducted into the New York Art Directors Club Hall of Fame.

173

Armin Hofmann
Born in Winterthur, 1920. Grew up during
the great era of Swiss graphic design.
Works in Basle, where he began his career
as a teacher at the School of Design
in 1946, and continued to teach there for
over forty years. He has also been visiting
lecturer at the Museum College of Art,
Philadelphia, visiting professor at the
National Design Institute, Ahmedabad,
India and Director of the Yale Summer
Program, Brissago.

Takenobu Igarashi
Began working as a graphic designer
in Tokyo in 1970. Worked on numerous
corporate identity design programmes,
and since the 1980s has also been working
on product design and sculpture, notably
designing graphics and products for the
New York Museum of Modern Art's store.
He now works mainly at his Los Angeles
studio, using the computer in his designs
and sculpture.

Herbert W. Kapitzki
Born 1925. Freelance graphic designer
since 1953. Lecturer and head of
department, Hochschule für Gestaltung,
Ulm, 1964-68. Professor at the Berlin
Hoschschule der Künste since 1970.
Founder of the Ulm "Forum for Design".

Burton Kramer
Educated at Yale University and the
Institute of Design, Chicago. Principal
of Kramer Design Associates Ltd, Toronto,
Academician of the Royal Canadian
Academy of Arts, and Fellow of the
Graphic Designers of Canada.

Mervyn Kurlansky
Educated at London's Central School
of Art. Started his own practice in 1961,
became head of graphics at Knoll
International's Planning Unit in 1962,
joined Crosby/Fletcher/Forbes in 1969
and was co-founder of Pentagram in 1972.
His accolades include Designers and Art
Directors Association Silver Awards,
a Gold Award from Japan's Ministry of
Trade and Industry, and awards from the
New York Art Directors Club.

Roger Law
Co-creator of the immensely influential
television series *Spitting Image*, which
uses caricature puppets in a satirical
mode. He may not have elevated caricature
to the level of fine art but no one has done
more to broaden its appeal.

Laurence Madrelle
Works in Paris, with a team of five
designers, on subjects related to the
citizen rather than the consumer.

Enzo Mari
Born 1932. Italian artist and designer,
with numerous publications and exhibitions
to his credit.

Les Mason
Born in California, 1924. Studied at the
Chouinard Institute and gained wide
recognition for his work with West Coast
Designers before moving to Melbourne,
Australia in 1961. Ran his own studio for
many years before moving to Perth, where
he now divides his time between design,
painting and printmaking. Has won many
awards both locally and internationally for
design and typography.

Shin Matsunaga
Born in Tokyo, 1949. Established Shin
Matsunaga Design Inc. in 1971. Received
Gold and Honorary Award of the 12th
International Poster Biennale, Warsaw.

Katherine McCoy
Senior Lecturer at Illinois Institute
of Technology's Institute of Design in
Chicago, and a Visiting Professor of
the Royal College of Art, London. Was
co-chairman of the Design Department at
Cranbrook Academy of Art for twenty-three
years. Besides her own practice, McCoy &
McCoy Associates, she is president of the
American Center for Design, and a Fellow
and past president of the Industrial
Designers Society of America.

Fernando Medina
Born in Spain. Has lived and worked in Madrid, Montreal, Tokyo and Los Angeles over the last twenty-five years, currently dividing his time between Madrid and New York. Work seen in the CN Pavilion at Expo '86, Vancouver; Neocon 22, Chicago; MOMA, New York; Expo '92, Seville.

Bruno Monguzzi
Born in Tessin, Switzerland in 1941. Studied in Geneva and London. Joined Studio Boggeri in the early 1960s. Combines commissions for graphic, editorial and exhibition design with teaching positions in Italy, Switzerland and the USA.

Kazumasa Nagai
Born in 1929. President of JAGDA and CEO of Nippon Design Centre Inc. Gold Prize in Warsaw Biennale 1966 and Grand Prix in Brno Biennale 1988.

Josep Pla-Narbona
Born in Barcelona, 1928. Studied at the Academy of Arts, spent time in Paris (1956-58) and the USA (1969-72). Independent graphic designer since 1960. Turning towards drawing, etching, sculpture and lately also to painting.

Gérard Paris-Clavel
Born 1943. One of the founders of Grapus and l'Epicerie d'art frais (Fresh Art Grocery). Presently working freelance and with the "Ne Pas Plier" conspiracy, from Ivry-sur-Seine. "Father and citizen, seeks sound professional relationship, Utopia required, free quotation."

Tullio Pericoli
Born in the Italian Marches and lives in Milan. Has a worldwide reputation as a portrait-painter and artist. Works exhibited in many major international collections.

Michael Peters OBE
Graduated MFA from Yale, 1964. Worked for CBS Television in New York and set up Michael Peters and Partners in 1970, firm quoted on the London Stock Exchange. Awarded OBE for services to design in 1990. Created Identica (1992), a new design and communications consultancy linked to a science and technology centre in Cambridge. Has won numerous awards and is particularly interested in the role of design in the prediction of future trends.

Jan Rajlich
Born in Dírná, Czechoslovakia, 1920. Studied at the Art College of Zlín, 1939-44. Has been living in Brno since 1950, working as a freelance graphic designer and painter, much involved in the field of education. In 1963 founded the International Biennale of Graphic Design in Brno, and until 1992 was regularly involved in its organization.

Paula Scher
Trained as an illustrator at the Tyler School of Art in Philadelphia, then worked for CBS records for ten years, designing posters and record sleeves. Built her practice and reputation at her New York consultancy, Koppel and Scher, then joined Pentagram as a partner in 1991. She has received hundreds of design awards and her work is represented in major collections including MOMA, New York and the Centre Georges Pompidou, Paris.

Helmut Schmid
Austrian-born German designer currently working in Osaka, Japan on bilingual/bi-scriptural design concepts. Studied under Emil Ruder and Kurt Hauert in Basel, Switzerland. Edited and designed *typography today* (Tokyo, 1980).

Henry Steiner
Born in Vienna 1934; raised in New York; MFA Yale, 1957; Fulbright to the Sorbonne, 1958-60. Founded Steiner & Co. (formerly Graphic Communication Ltd) in Hong Kong, 1964; author with Ken Hass, of *Cross-Cultural Design.*

175

Deborah Sussman
Has wanted a double career as an artist
and actress ever since she can remember,
and acted in college as well as in the
Yiddish theatre for a short while. Thinks the
duel career suited her Gemini personality.

Niklaus Troxler
Born in Willisau, Switzerland, 1947.
Studied typesetting and graphic design
at the Lucerne Art School, then worked
as an art director in Paris. Started his own
graphic design studio in 1973, specializing
in poster design. Has won many competitions and awards, including the Special
Prize at the Poster Biennale, Warsaw
(1990), Silver Medal at the Brno Biennale
(1990), and the ICOGRADA Excellence
Award (1992).

Wolfgang Weingart
Born in 1941, trained as a lead typesetter.
Since 1968 he has taught typography at
the Basel School of Design, and lectured
extensively abroad. Founder of the period-
icals *TM/communications* and *Typographic
Process.*

Benno Wissing
Born in Holland, 1922. Trained as an
architect before going into graphic design.
As a former partner in Total Design,
Amsterdam, was responsible for the sign
system at Amsterdam's Schiphol airport
(the first comprehensive sign system
at any airport). Freelances in Holland and
the USA, where he has an office in
Providence. Has taught at the Rhode Island
School of Design.

Henry Wolf
Born in Vienna, 1925. Settled in the USA in
1941. Art director, designer, teacher, writer
and photographer. Recipient of innumerable
awards and honours, including the AIGA
Gold Medal; inducted into the New York
Art Directors Club Hall of Fame.

INDEX

183